GREAT PRO QUARTERBACKS

Edited and with an Introduction by
LUD DUROSKA

Written by members of *The New York Times* Sports Staff

GROSSET & DUNLAP • Publishers • New York
A National General Company

Dedicated with love
to Martha,
my favorite quarterback

Acknowledgment

The cooperation of the National Football League staff, especially Joe Browne, and of the PR directors of the teams for whom the great pro quarterbacks played, or play, is gratefully acknowledged.

Thanks to John Looney and Fred Cantey for their assistance in photo research.

Passing records were supplied by the Elias Sports Bureau, official statisticians for the National Football League.

Library of Congress Catalog Card Number: 78–158762

ISBN: 0-448-02084-X (Trade Edition)
ISBN: 0-448-03792-0 (Library Edition)

Contents

Introduction

Even though its first major league was not organized until 1920—some seven decades after baseball—pro football has climbed so spectacularly in fan interest that it is now indisputably the national pastime. (Contrary to popular impression, its original name was not the National Football League. When the founding fathers, including George Halas, the perennial Papa of the Chicago Bears, met on that fall day in the auto dealer's showroom in Canton, Ohio, they christened their fledgling group the American Professional Football Association. Two seasons and 21 months later the name was changed to the National Football League.)

But it was not until 1933 that the forward pass was permitted to be thrown from any place behind the line of scrimmage, the same year that the goal posts were moved up to the goal line. Both rule changes were made in the hope of "opening up" the game by making scoring easier. Previously, the pass was very much in the shadow of the run as an attacking weapon, so much so that coaches frowned upon passing on any down except third. Talented passers, such as Benny Friedman of Michigan, Arnie Herber of Colorado, Harry Newman of Michigan, and Cecil Isbell of Purdue, continued to be standouts when they entered the pro ranks. However, the formations of that day (basically, the single wing and the double wing) and the thinking of bench pundits hindered the full use of their abilities.

In 1937 George Preston Marshall transferred the Boston Redskins to Washington, D.C. Of more historic import was the fact that Marshall had signed Sammy Baugh, acclaimed for his feats at Texas Christian University as the finest collegiate passer in many years. Baugh immediately lived up to his reputation and led the Redskins to the NFL championship in his rookie season. Of all the great pro quarterbacks who followed him, none fitted in so easily and became an established star so quickly. The only other great pro quarterback who piloted his team to league honors in his first year was Otto Graham of the Cleveland Browns. But, as he so rightfully has pointed out, his debut was under vastly different circumstances. All the other players in his league were also pro rookies in 1946, the year the All-American Conference opened shop for the first time.

As sports writers are wont to say, Baugh "revolutionized" the game with his extraordinary passing skills. In truth, he may likely have been the greatest pro quarterback. A common accolade: "Sammy can throw long and short. He can zip the ball in and he can 'pull the string' (throw softly). He can hit his man at any spot on the field and at any speed. He can do it all." Elderly experts who were on the scene in the 1920's and 1930's—and therefore have observed all the great passers—are inclined to agree.

One more historic development had to occur before the quarterback became the preeminent performer on the gridiron. That was the popularization of the T-formation, which was nearly as old as football itself. Amos Alonzo Stagg had employed the T-formation at the University of Chicago as long ago as the early 1890's. He was to have a local disciple by the name of George Halas. When he formed his first professional team, the Decatur Staleys (who were to become the Bears), in 1920, Halas used the T-formation. But the pro pioneer was alone in his preference for the formation in which the quarterback handled the ball on every play. The other NFL teams ignored the T until the Bears rocked the football world in 1940 with their 73–0 rout of the Redskins. Then the NFL coaches scrambled to switch over to the T. Within ten years every pro team except the Pittsburgh Steelers had converted, and they finally capitulated in 1952.

The result today can be shown by the following comparisons: Henry Aaron bats four times a game; Tom Seaver pitches every fourth day; Kareem Abdul-Jabbar shoots about one-quarter of his team's field-goal attempts. That's the maximum they—or any other stars in their sports—contribute to the success of their teams. By contrast, any pro quarterback starts and actively takes part in every offensive play of every game, except for kicking situations. He knows each blocking assignment for his ten teammates (let him get sacked and he can tell immediately which one failed him). He is expected to recognize the shifting and camouflaged defensive alignments and react accordingly. He is supposed to ignore pain and wounds and the momentary clouding of the brain from his last jolting encounter with a defender to think clearly and call the best play, given the strategic considerations. He is also supposed to inspire his teammates to victory. And, of course, when he isn't handing off the ball, he is passing—the special skill that got him the job in the first place. In no other team sport does one player have to know so much and carry so much responsibility (and also get beat up in the bargain without being able to retaliate).

For these reasons the pro quarterback is the most highly paid and the most publicized of football players. And that is why the fan is most familiar and most interested in him. And why this book was created. In prose and pictures, here are the great pro quarterbacks . . . at least, in one man's opinion.

Lud Duroska

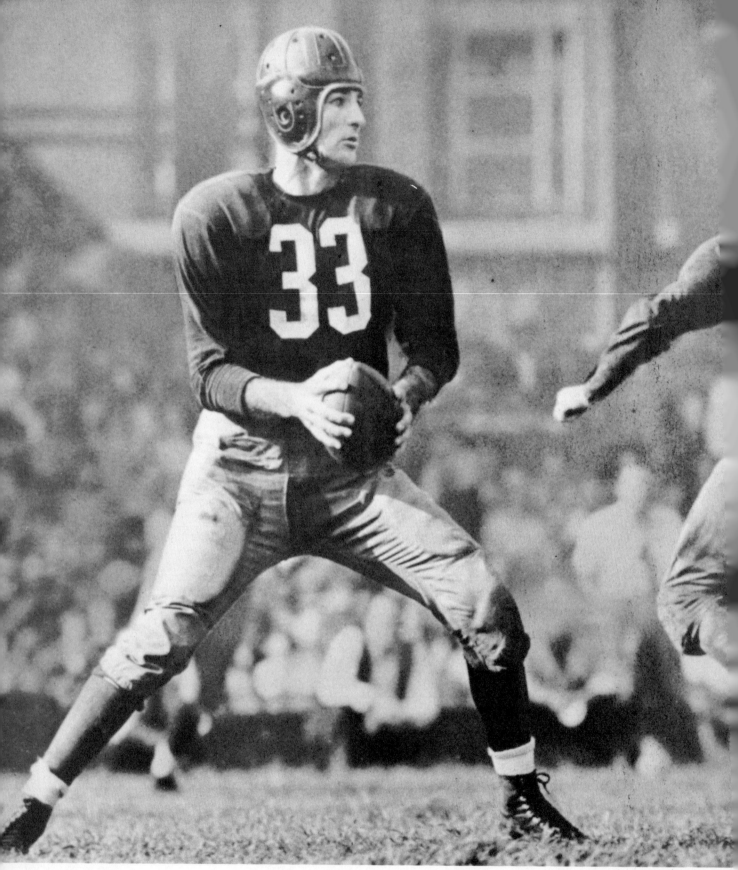

Ready to throw the ball as the linemen carry on their private battles.

Sammy Baugh

Sammy Baugh

by Joseph Durso

In the days of the 60-minute player, Baugh, also outstanding on defense, crouches to stop Dave Smukler of Eagles.

His name was Samuel Adrian Baugh, and he was a six-foot-two-inch right-hander from Texas who sometimes weighed as much as 180 pounds, who always spoke with a drawl, and who never wore cowboy boots or a ten-gallon hat. Never, that is, until the day in 1937 that he flew into Washington, D.C., wearing both. He was the rookie quarterback for the Washington Redskins that day, and he had a problem: his feet were hurting inside the new boots.

He was wearing them because the owner of the team, George Preston Marshall, was determined that his new quarterback would arrive on the pro football scene with all the trappings of a Texan. And Sammy Baugh was a Texan, all right—straight out of places like Temple, where he was born on March 17, 1914; Sweetwater, where he

Baugh leaps and stiff-arms Bill Osmanski of Bears in 1943 NFL championship game.

played end on the high school team; and Fort Worth, where he attended Texas Christian University because the baseball coach felt certain he could make the big leagues as a third baseman.

But when Marshall met him in the capital that day in 1937, the tall Texan ached from the confines of those cowboy boots with pointed toes. He didn't know it at the time, but life in the National Football League threatened to be even more confining. It was a rough-and-tough league that had evolved over twenty years, bruise by bruise, and it had been built on conservative theories: No team passed from inside its own 25-yard line, it was acceptable to pass on third down for the next 50 yards, and the choice was left to the quarterback only inside the other team's 25.

Yet, for the next sixteen seasons, the lanky slinger from the Panhandle survived in an absolutely hostile business and pitched the Redskins to five division titles and two league championships. Not only that, but he once completed 18 of 21 passes against the Pittsburgh Steelers; one season he completed seventy percent of his passes; he led the league in punting five times, averaging almost 60 yards a kick in one game and 51 yards a kick in one season; and he finished with 1,709 completions for 22,085 yards—which is thirteen miles, even in Texas. And as if that weren't enough for one sixty-minute man, he intercepted four passes on defense one day against the Detroit Lions.

In other words, he was something new in football. His roundabout route to pro football started in the days just after World War I, when he was growing up in Texas and the NFL was growing up in the obscure gridirons of the Middle West.

Those were the days when the United States was rebounding from the war into the Roaring Twenties; the days of the Barrymores on Broadway, Tex Rickard at Madison Square Garden, John McGraw at the Polo Grounds in New York, and Babe Ruth at Yankee Stadium. And in Green Bay, Wisconsin, a businessman named Frank Peck and a fullback named Earle Louis ("Curly") Lambeau, fresh out of Notre Dame, were piecing together a football team.

They started with $500 that Peck contributed from the Indian Packing Company, which he owned, with instructions to Lambeau to "equip" a team. Lambeau had been the captain of Green Bay's East High School team in 1916 and 1917 and Notre Dame's fullback in 1918. Now he was working for Peck's packing company, making $250 a month, and had $500 to buy sweaters and stockings.

"We played for the love of the game," he recalled. "We agreed to split any money we got and each man was to pay his own doctor bills."

At the end of the first season, when they had passed the hat for the last time and paid the doctors' bills for the last time, each of the regulars pocketed $16.75. It wasn't much, any way you sliced it, but professional football had arrived in Green Bay.

Ten years later, as the twenties slipped into the thirties and the Great Depression pervaded the country, they no longer passed the hat at pro football games. The team played to a lot of empty seats on Sunday afternoons. The sport, nevertheless, was kept alive by such players as Red Grange, Ernie Nevers, and Ken Strong, and the players in turn were kept alive professionally by such owners as George Halas, Art Rooney, Tim Mara, Bert Bell, and George Preston Marshall.

Meanwhile, back at the ranch, the Baughs of Temple, Texas, were moving to Sweetwater, and it was there that Sammy

Wide World
Baugh frustrates Chicago Cardinals' rushers by getting pass away.

15

made his mark—as a baseball prospect. The coach from Texas Christian University, Dutch Meyer, got a look at him in high school and went back to the college to exult to the football coach, Francis (Close-the-Gates-of-Mercy) Schmidt:

"I just saw a great baseball player, a kid named Baugh. I sure could use him on our club. I understand he also plays a little football at Sweetwater. Do you think we could get him in here with a football scholarship?"

"Okay," replied the obliging Schmidt, "but I sure wish we could have gotten his teammate, Red Sheridan. It's a shame he went to Texas."

Neither Schmidt nor Meyer, who also doubled as the freshman football coach, spent much time mourning the loss of Sheridan, once they got a look at Baugh throwing passes. The following year, when Baugh became a sophomore, Meyer succeeded Schmidt as varsity football coach.

That was the start of Baugh's football career. Meyer immediately put him to work pitching passes, and Baugh made 599 in three seasons for 274 completions, 3,439 yards, and 39 touchdowns. He also did some fancy punting, notably in the Sugar Bowl in his junior year when he kicked 14 times, averaged 50 yards, and even set up the winning field goal on a wet turf as TCU edged past Louisiana State with the grudging score of 3–2.

The last two seasons in college, he made all-American, but he still had a hankering for baseball, and signed with the St. Louis Cardinals after graduating in 1937. They switched him from third base to shortstop—to give that good right arm longer range—and gave him a whirl of the farm system: Sacramento, Columbus, Rochester. But he had trouble hitting the curve ball and another rookie shortstop, Marty Marion, didn't. So the temptation was growing to switch back to football, when along

came George Preston Marshall, who had just moved the Redskins from Boston to Washington and was looking for an outstanding player. He offered Baugh $5,000, and the following January "Slingin' Sam" descended the steps of the airplane, reporting to the Redskins with his ten-gallon hat, cowboy boots, and aching feet.

He became an instant success by any criterion. The Redskins started to pack the customers into the ballpark, turning an $85,000 deficit into a $20,000 profit in one season. At one point they were able to chalk up forty sellouts in a row. Artistically, Baugh made history of sorts before the season even began. In the annual All-Star Game at Chicago, he threw a touchdown pass to Gaynell Tinsley of LSU to beat the Green Bay Packers, 6–0, and for the first time in the series the college boys survived a confrontation with the professional champions.

When the regular season opened, the Redskins competed with the hard-nosed New York Giants. Result: 11 completions in 16 passes for the new boy on the block, and a 13–3 victory for the 'Skins. Three months later, they went all the way to the Eastern title with a 49–14 drubbing of the Giants in the Polo Grounds, with Baugh firing 11-for-15 against the best defense in the league. In the league championship game against the Chicago Bears, he passed 42 yards to running back Cliff Battles from his own end zone. He later threw three touchdown passes, leading the Redskins to a 28–21 decision and the title.

For the next ten seasons, the Redskins stayed in the black both financially and statistically in the league standings. And their quarterback stayed in the black, too, earning something like $300,000 during his career, while some players were still being paid "per game." In fact, at one time Baugh was paid at the rate of $727 a game, and he raised eyebrows around the league by holding out for an annual retainer that was rumored to be somewhere between $13,000 and $25,000.

"Whoever heard of me getting $25,-000?" Baugh asked. "It's the bunk—just publicity. Salaries just don't come that high in professional football. The amount I earned in my first year was very good for a youngster. It's tough going, though—having those big fellows slam you around after every pass. I guess I earned that money."

Then he turned sly, hinted that he'd rather sign at the old per-game rate—say, for three years—and said, "For one year's football, $13,000 or $14,000 is considerable money, but I'm a pretty frail boy, you know, and I'm likely to go out any time. Suppose I signed for a one-year term and got hurt. I'd be through. Under terms of the three-year contract, I am protecting myself for that length of time—broken leg, smashed career or not."

Sammy proved as quick with a bon mot as with a dollar. In his first blackboard drill with Coach Ray Flaherty, he was instructed, "And when your receiver reaches this point, I want you to hit him in the eye." Not too intimidated, the rookie replied impertinently, "Which eye?"

Another time, he listened to a prolonged chalk-talk briefing, complete with diagrams and equations, and observed, "The algebra teacher used to be the football coach; now the football coach is the algebra teacher."

Another time, he addressed a gathering of FBI men and opened with, "This is the most protection I've had all year."

But his most quoted quip came after a game on December 8, 1940, when the Bears finally avenged themselves for past defeats and even a few insults from the Redskins. Not only had they lost the title three years earlier to Washington in Baugh's rookie season, but they also had

Baugh, also one of the best NFL punters, booms one against Bears in 1942.

lost a 7–3 battle to them a few weeks earlier. And Marshall had baited George Halas after that game by calling the Bears "a first-half team" and "a bunch of crybabies."

Halas wasted no time posting newspaper clippings containing such tidbits on the Bears' locker room wall, and when the teams met in Griffith Stadium in the return match, the Bears wasted no time settling an old score: Bill Osmanski ran 68 yards for a touchdown on the second play of the game.

The clippings on the wall were now replaced by the handwriting on the wall, and the handwriting was done by some tough cookies. Sid Luckman was the Chicago quarterback, Osmanski the fullback, George McAfee the halfback. The line in-

Baugh fires pass to Ward Cuff of Giants in a snowy All-Star game in 1942.

cluded Ken Kavanaugh, Lee Artoe, Ed Kolman, Joe Stydahar, and Bulldog Turner.

By the end of the first half, the toll was 28–0, and if George Marshall really believed the Bears were a first-half team, his beliefs were about to be shattered. They added seven more touchdowns in the second half, en route to a 73–0 bulldozing of the Redskins, who lost the title in a record rout.

When it was over, the 36,034 spectators were as shocked as the Redskins, whose quarterback sat silently in front of his locker trying to answer the unanswerable questions thrown his way by the sportswriters. If one of his early passes had been caught in the end zone by Charley Malone, one asked, would there have been a difference in the outcome?

"Yes, there would have been a difference," Baugh conceded. "The score would have been 73–7."

.Two years later, in a less memorable game, the Redskins returned the favor by upsetting the Bears for the league title, 14–6. Baugh, now a sixth-year man who played the full sixty minutes regardless of who had the ball, tipped the balance with an 83-yard punt after a fake pass. When Luckman tried to pass his way out of the hole, the Redskins intercepted, and then Baugh hit Wilbur Moore with a 32-yard touchdown pass for a 7–6 lead.

In the third quarter, when the Bears dropped back on defense to protect against Baugh's passes, he kept the ball on the ground for twelve straight plays and another touchdown for the championship.

It was the last championship that Baugh had a hand in. The following year he was out of the title game most of the time (because of a concussion) and the big bad Bears whipped Washington. And in 1945, after the Redskins had switched from the single-wing to the T-formation, they lost a wintry playoff game to the Cleveland Rams, 15–14.

A whole new postwar era was beginning now, and with it came a new generation of football players, including quarterbacks. But Baugh, in his eleventh season, in 1947, still had a few parting shots left in his rifle. He fired a few of them against the Chicago Cardinals one afternoon in Washington, just after the hometown fans had treated him to "Baugh Day," a sort of salute to the Old Guard. The Old Guard responded with 25 completions for 355 yards and six touchdowns.

Five years later he fired a few more memorable shots as time ran out on his pro career. He now was a part-time quarterback and a full-time teacher of Eddie LeBaron, the jockey-sized quarterback from the College of the Pacific. They alternated behind the center until Baugh injured his right hand in training, but when they opened the season against the Cardinals, the 38-year-old veteran was the starting pitcher.

It was his last hour on the stage, and he made the most of it. Working under heavy pressure from the Cardinal line, he com-

pleted nine straight passes, then a tenth, just as the 255-pound Don Joyce barreled into him. Baugh picked himself up from the ground, feeling pain up to his right shoulder, and fired his eleventh completion in a row. As he did, Joyce smashed into him again, and suddenly they were throwing punches.

It was Baugh's first and last fight on the field, and he paid for it with his first and last heave-ho from the officials. It was also his final appearance as a quarterback: sixteen years, 2,995 passes, 186 touchdowns, and 338 punts after he started.

Afterward, he divided his time between his 6,000-acre ranch in Texas and coaching jobs at Hardin-Simmons College in Abilene, and with the New York Titans and the Houston Oilers.

He had worn out sixty pairs of football shoes and a hundred jerseys doing his thing as the best in the business, and he had survived sixteen seasons of playing quarterback on offense and safetyman on defense. But what football fans remember is the tall man wearing No. 33 on his jersey, dropping back to pass.

Year	Team	Games	Att.	Comp.	Pct.	Yards	TDs	Long	Int.	Pct. Int.	Avg. Gain
1937	Wash.	11	171	81	47.4	1127	7	59	14	8.2	6.59
1938	Wash.	10	128	63	49.2	853	5	60	11	8.6	6.66
1939	Wash.	8	96	53	55.2	518	6	44	9	9.4	5.40
1940	Wash.	11	177	111	62.7	1367	12	t81	10	5.6	7.72
1941	Wash.	11	193	106	54.9	1236	10	55	19	9.8	6.40
1942	Wash.	11	225	132	58.7	1524	16	53	11	4.9	6.77
1943	Wash.	10	239	133	55.6	1754	23	t72	19	7.9	7.34
1944	Wash.	8	146	82	56.2	849	4	t71	8	5.5	5.82
1945	Wash.	10	182	128	70.3	1669	11	t70	4	2.2	9.17
1946	Wash.	9	161	87	54.0	1163	8	t51	17	10.6	7.22
1947	Wash.	12	354	210	59.3	2938	25	t74	15	4.2	8.30
1948	Wash.	12	315	185	58.7	2599	22	86	23	7.3	8.25
1949	Wash.	12	255	145	56.9	1903	18	76	14	5.5	7.46
1950	Wash.	9	166	90	54.2	1130	10	56	11	6.6	6.81
1951	Wash.	11	154	67	43.5	1104	7	53	17	11.0	7.17
1952	Wash.	4	33	20	60.6	152	2	20	1	3.0	4.61
Totals 16 yrs.		**159**	**2995**	**1693**	**56.5**	**21,886**	**186**	**86**	**203**	**6.8**	**7.31**

Breaks into clear and scores in 1943 championship game against Bears.

Sid Luckman

Sid Luckman
by Sam Goldaper

George Halas, the coach of the Chicago Bears, once said of Sid Luckman: "I don't think I can ever recall a game where Sid called the wrong play. Having this fellow at quarterback was the equivalent of having another coach on the field. He was the greatest play-director I have ever seen."

Brooklyn-born and Columbia-educated, Luckman was gentlemanly, modest and kindly off the field, but unyielding and very talented on it.

Passing has always been the chief asset of a T-formation quarterback, but Luckman's skills did not end with his arm. He was an excellent punter, a punishing blocker, and an effective tackler. But most of all, he was a leader who played the key role in revamping pro football's modern offense.

Luckman starred on a dozen Sunday af-

Typical example of how Bears dominated Redskins in 73-0 rout for 1940 title as Luckman tackles Jimmy Johnston and other teammates dash over to help out.

22

ternoons a year from 1939 through 1950, with time out in 1944 to serve in the U.S. merchant marine during World War II. Without Luckman the Bears still would have been big and bad, but not necessarily winners. With him they won four National Football League championships and Luckman wrote his name into football history as the first of the great T-formation quarterbacks.

During his twelve seasons, Luckman was selected all-league quarterback six times. In 1940, his first full season at quarterback, he led the Chicago Bears when they overwhelmed the Washington Redskins, 73–0, for the most humiliating defeat ever inflicted in a pro championship game. Three seasons later, he was named the league's most valuable player after he threw seven touchdown passes against the New York Giants—a record that has been equaled but never surpassed.

Once, while watching Luckman cradle the ball, scan the field for receivers, and carefully watch for onrushing tacklers, a Chicago newspaperman remarked, "Luckman makes it look so easy—he looks like he's playing catch in the backyard."

Perhaps the most remarkable thing about Luckman's success was his complete adaptability to a strange offensive formation. When he arrived in 1939, the Chicago Bears were the only pro team using a T-formation. Luckman had been a halfback in Columbia's version of the single wing. George Halas' selection of a single-wing halfback to run a T-formation was surprising. His selection of Luckman was just as surprising.

College football in 1938 had produced an outstanding crop of brilliant senior backs. The consensus all-Americans were Marshall Goldberg of Pittsburgh, Vic Bottari of California, Davey O'Brien of Texas Christian, and Bob MacLeod of Dartmouth. Only one of the six all-American

teams had Luckman in the backfield.

That year the Bears traded Edgar ("Eggs") Manske, an end, to Pittsburgh in exchange for the rights to the Steelers' top draft choice. Since Pittsburgh finished last, the Bears had the pick of the nation's top collegians.

Everyone expected George Halas to select O'Brien, who had broken all of Sammy Baugh's passing records at TCU. Instead, Halas surprised the experts and picked Luckman. He explained the selection as "a hunch, more than anything else." That was difficult to believe, because the Bears had the best scouting system and Halas had been a frequent spectator at Luckman's games at Columbia University. Once, when Halas saw Syracuse beat Columbia, 13–12, he turned to Bob Harron, the Columbia sports publicist, and said, "There's a boy I'd like to have on my club."

During Luckman's three years at Columbia, his team was seldom in the national spotlight, but Luckman showed himself to be an outstanding passer, and Halas considered him a brilliant strategist.

At first, Sid did not consider playing professionally. But what Halas described as "one of the most attractive contracts we have ever offered to a freshman player," coupled with Luckman's decision to marry, changed Luckman's mind. He reportedly signed for $10,000 a year, a lot of money in those days.

Halas, impatient for Luckman to be schooled in the T-formation, arranged for him to come to Chicago two weeks before he was scheduled to play for the College All-Stars against the New York Giants. Halas assigned Lucas Johnsos, an aide, the task of educating Luckman. He insisted that Sid familiarize himself with the duties of the other three backs. He also wanted him to know the blocking assignments of every lineman on every play.

As a pupil, Luckman was eager and apt.

Tom Fears cuts across field to try to prevent Luckman from scoring a touchdown.

Luckman and George Halas, owner of Bears, studying Chicago's play diagrams.

After practice he would go home and rehearse his faking and pivoting in front of a mirror. He wasn't satisfied until he could almost fool himself.

Some of the Bears' plays shocked Luckman in the beginning. At Columbia, Coach Lou Little meticulously massed blockers in front of the ball carriers. When Johnsos outlined plays in which the ball carriers went through a quick opening in the line unescorted, Luckman protested.

"Gosh, Luke," said Luckman, "if those halfbacks go through the line alone, they'll get killed."

"Don't worry, Sid," said Luke. "As fast as they get killed, we'll send in new ones."

In his first season, Luckman broke in gradually. George Halas had planned to use him more as a pass-throwing halfback than as a quarterback. When Billy Patterson, whom Halas had counted on to be the No. 2 quarterback, failed to master the ball-handling assignments, Luckman was forced into action.

Sid Luckman set no world on fire in his rookie season. He played in all eleven games, but tossed only 51 passes, completed 23 for 636 yards. Davey O'Brien's season was far better, although his team, the Philadelphia Eagles, won once in eleven games. He was named to the All-Star team after he set three records and completed 99 of 201 passes for 1,324 yards.

But Halas did not regret his selection of Luckman over O'Brien. When the Brooklyn Dodgers offered him $15,000 for Sid's contract, he shook his head and said, "He's not for sale or trade. Take my word for it and watch this boy go from now on."

Halas knew something that the records of the 1939 season failed to show. "In all my years in football," he said, "I've never seen a player who worked as hard as Luckman. When others left the practice field, he stayed on. He practiced ball-handling, pivoting, and faking by the hour. He became great at it because he put in about four hundred percent more effort than the average athlete was willing to devote."

Halas' prediction of Luckman's future fame came true during the 1940 season when Sid Luckman blossomed into one of the NFL's brightest stars. He led the Bears to the Western Division title with an 8–3 record. One of the defeats was a 7–3 controversial loss to the Washington Redskins. Chicago had complained that on the final play of the game pass interference had not been called on Frank Filchock, preventing a Bears' score.

Washington Redskins' owner George Marshall taunted Chicago, "They're strictly a first-half team. They give up."

When Washington won the Western Division title, the Bears got a rematch. Halas prepared for the rematch game which Washington was favored to win. Every hostile remark by Marshall or a Redskin player printed in the newspapers was prominently displayed in the Chicago dressing room. At the same time, the Bears did their homework well. Halas made his team watch movies of that first Redskin game again and again.

"You could almost sense that something tremendous was going to happen that day as we assembled for the trip to Washington," said Luckman.

On the first play of the game, Luckman used a standard off-tackle run. He discovered that the Redskins' defense was unaltered from their earlier meeting. Sid faked to Ray Nolting on the second play, but handed off to Bill Osmanski, who went over left guard and raced 68 yards for a touchdown. Chicago scored twice more in the first quarter, once in the second, four times in the third, and three times in the fourth . . . and the 73–0 massacre was part of pro football history.

Although Luckman played only thirty minutes, he was the key to the Bears' victory. *The New York Times,* in its report of the game, stated, "No field general ever called plays more artistically. He was letter-perfect."

The four seasons that followed were outstanding ones for Luckman and the Bears. During that time, he became the complete master of the T-formation and led Chicago to three Western Division championships and two NFL titles. In 1941, 1942, 1943, and 1944, he was named to the All-Star team. He completed 110 passes out of 202 attempts for a record-breaking 2,194 yards and 28 touchdowns in 1943. Sid was the first Chicago Bear player ever to win the Most Valuable Player award.

Bob Snyder, Luckman's understudy at quarterback, who later coached the Los Angeles Rams, paid Sid this tribute as a play-caller: "Sid can sit down and draw you every blocking assignment of the other ten Bears from each of the vast repertoire of plays the Bears used. He knew exactly what every one of his teammates was supposed to do, and it didn't matter if the assignments were against five-, six-, or seven-men lines."

What Luckman has called his greatest day as passer came on November 14, 1943. The place was the Polo Grounds. The opposing team was the New York Giants. The day had been advertised as "Luckman Day." More than 50,000 fans, many of whom had watched Sid play at Columbia and at Erasmus Hall High School in Brooklyn, turned out to pay tribute.

Luckman gave them a memorable day. He threw seven touchdown passes against the Giants, who were tied for the Eastern Conference lead at the time. The Giants were coached by Steve Owen, who had come up with an "umbrella defense" which placed four men in a perimeter. At the time it was judged to be the best defense against the passing game. But there was no defense against Luckman on "his day."

A few weeks earlier, Sammy Baugh of the Washington Redskins had established a game record of six touchdown passes. On "his day," Luckman's assault on Baugh's record started almost immediately. Luckman hit Jim Benton with a 4-yard touchdown pass. He threw a spectacular 44-yard pass to Connie Berry for the second score and No. 3 went to Hampton Pool from 27 yards out.

The next touchdown was the only one that Chicago did not score on a pass. Harry Clark ran four yards for the touchdown after a long Luckman pass had set it up.

Luckman produced his fourth scoring pass, a 33-yarder, to Clark, then hit Benton again for a touchdown. When he flipped

Five Bears who starred together receive plaques as "History Makers of Football." From left: Joe Stydahar, Ray Nolting, Luckman, Bill Osmanski, George McAfee.

a pass to George Wilson over the middle for his sixth touchdown toss, he matched Baugh's performance.

At this point, the Bears were leading, 42–7. When the coaches tried taking Sid out of the game, the crowd and Sid's teammates, thinking of the record, objected strenuously.

"Let him go for it," they said. "This is his day."

And Luckman, late in the game, got his record by passing to Pool, who made an acrobatic catch for the touchdown. Luckman had his seven touchdown passes and the Bears had a 56–7 victory. That afternoon, Sid threw for 433 yards, and Owen

must have wondered about his "umbrella defense."

Sid had many other great moments. One of them was the 1943 championship game against the Washington Redskins. The pregame prediction of sportswriters was that the passing of Luckman and Baugh "would darken the skies." The expected battle never developed. The Bears had little trouble winning, 41–21, with Luckman connecting for five touchdown passes. Baugh, who threw for two touchdowns, was out of action for most of the afternoon after a collision with Luckman. Baugh was shaken up when he tried tackling Luckman after Sid had fielded a punt.

"I took his punt near the sideline," said Luckman, "and they had one man coming at me from one side and another from the other side. There was nothing left for me to do but go straight through. I saw Baugh ahead of me.

"He was running full speed. I got my knees pumping as hard as I could. So, going full speed, we came straight at each other. He dove at me, head on, and as my left knee went down, my right knee hit him on the forehead. He fell back and I went on over him."

During most of 1944 and for part of the following season, Luckman served in the U.S. merchant marine. Upon his return, the Bears lost five straight games and he threw for only two touchdowns. He seriously considered retiring. Clark Shaughnessy, who served as the Bears' advisory coach, talked him out of it. Sid went "back to work" and in the next three games made a strong comeback, passing for eight touchdowns. It was a rejuvenated Luckman who led the NFL in pass completions in 1946 and the Bears to their fourth championship in seven years.

Chicago beat the Giants for the title, 24–14, before 61,000 fans at the Polo Grounds, and Luckman put on a masterful demonstration as a field general. He virtually abandoned the pass and relied on a ground attack. The climax came when he scored the clinching touchdown on a 19-yard bootleg play. It was the only time he had carried the ball all season.

Although Luckman played through the 1950 season, leading the league in completion percentage in 1947, his touchdown run against the Giants in 1946 might be considered the last of his great moments.

Johnny Lujack arrived for the 1948 season and the following year the former Notre Dame hero took over as the starting quarterback.

In 1950, at the age of 34 and nearing retirement, Sid Luckman asked George Halas to let him play against the Detroit Lions. The Bears' coach agreed. On the second play after Luckman entered the game, he called a pass. As he faded back, he was hit by a Lion and the ball was knocked loose. Detroit recovered the fumble and converted it into a touchdown.

As Luckman came off the field and headed for the Bears' bench, there were some boos and hisses, the first he had been subjected to in Chicago. As Sid sat bundled up in a blanket, Halas walked over to his side, hugged him and said, "Don't worry, son, you've done more than your share to make them happy."

Year	Team	Games	Att.	Comp.	Pct.	Yards	TDs	Long	Int.	Pct. Int.	Avg. Gain
1939	Chi.B.	11	51	23	45.1	636	5	62	4	7.8	12.47
1940	Chi.B.	11	105	48	45.7	941	6	57	9	8.6	8.96
1941	Chi.B.	11	119	68	57.1	1181	9	65	6	5.0	9.92
1942	Chi.B.	11	105	57	54.3	1023	10	57	12	11.4	9.74
1943	Chi.B.	10	202	110	54.5	2194	28	66	12	5.9	10.86
1944	Chi.B.	7	143	71	49.7	1018	11	t86	11	7.7	7.12
1945	Chi.B.	10	217	117	53.9	1725	14	t65	10	4.6	7.95
1946	Chi.B.	11	229	110	48.0	1826	17	48	16	7.0	7.97
1947	Chi.B.	12	323	176	54.5	2712	24	81	31	9.6	8.40
1948	Chi.B.	12	163	89	54.6	1047	13	53	14	8.6	6.42
1949	Chi.B.	8	50	22	44.0	200	1	34	3	6.0	4.00
1950	Chi.B.	7	37	13	35.1	180	1	44	2	5.4	4.86
Totals 12 yrs.		121	1744	904	51.8	14,683	139	t86	130	7.5	8.42

Heads into end zone for final touchdown of his career in 38-14 victory over Rams in 1955 championship game as blockers clear way.

Otto Graham

Otto Graham

by Thomas Rogers

I was born with good coordination," Otto Graham once remarked in a masterpiece of understatement. "But I worked for everything else I ever got out of sports. There is no shortcut to success. It takes practice. Too many kids like to think that because they have natural ability, they're going to be stars. But it doesn't work that way unless they're willing to work hard to polish the skill God gave them."

Otto Everett Graham, Jr. was one of the best polishers in the business. In his ten years as quarterback of the Cleveland Browns, his team reached the playoff ten times. With Graham, the Browns won four league crowns in the All-America Conference and three more in six National Football League championship games.

Although he was surrounded by other great athletes, such as Marion Motley, Lou

UPI
As a pro rookie in 1946 (left)

Graham, an underrated runner, sidesteps one Ram tackler but two others hem him in during 1955 title game Cleveland won.

Graham fakes handoff to
Ray Renfro . . .

takes off around Cleveland's
right end . . .

Groza, Danta Lavelli, Mac Speedie and Dub Jones, Graham was the man around whom Paul Brown built his dynasty. He was the first man signed by Brown in 1945, when the former Ohio State coach began putting together the unit that dominated its rivals from 1946 to 1955.

"The test of a quarterback is where his team finishes," said Brown at the end of Graham's career in 1955. "So Otto Graham, by that standard, was the best of all time."

In 1956, Cleveland's first year without Graham, the Browns had the first losing season in their history, an occurrence that underlined his importance.

Although Graham's statistical achievements were extraordinary—he completed 1,464 passes in 2,626 attempts for 23,584 yards and 174 touchdowns—there was more to his career than could be assessed by figures in a record book.

The six-foot-one-inch former tailback at Northwestern University combined a superb passing ability with a sometimes underrated skill as a runner, often turning broken-pass plays into substantial gains with long-striding jaunts through the defensive line.

Otto Graham's competitive fire was infectious to his teammates. A casually pleasant cockiness, which gave him a confident air, was a perfect complement to Coach Brown's tight-lipped austerity and precision. Both men were completely dedicated to winning and, though sometimes at odds about which particular play would best accomplish that purpose, together they created a mystique of victory for the Browns.

Four years of domination of the AAC spawned the tradition. The Browns lost only four games in four seasons, winning the league championship each time. But, although the team was considered the best by far of the 1946–1949 league, die-

eyes Los Angeles player
racing over . . .

and scores in 1955
championship game.

hard NFL backers doubted that the Browns could continue their winning tradition in the older, established league.

When the Browns, the Baltimore Colts, and the San Francisco 49ers were taken into the NFL for the 1950 season, Graham refused to admit that Cleveland was stepping into faster company.

"The AAC isn't defunct," he said with bland assurance at a Washington Touchdown Club banquet. "We simply absorbed the National League."

Graham and his teammates lived up to that remark in their first NFL season. They made their debut against the Philadelphia Eagles, who had won the league championship the previous two years—a matchup not made accidentally, so Cleveland fans believed.

"We would have played them for a barrel of beer or for nothing," said Graham. "Paul Brown didn't have to lift a finger or say one word to get us ready."

A crowd of 71,327 Eagle fans cheered their team and jeered the Browns when the Eagles took an early 3–0 lead on a 15-yard field goal by Cliff Patton.

But Graham responded with a series of short-yardage passes to Lavelli and Speedie that made Russ Craft, a Philadelphia defensive halfback, tighten his coverage and prepare for a long gainer, a 59-yard scoring pass to Jones.

Picking the Philadelphia secondary to pieces, Graham later threw scoring aerials to Lavelli and Speedie, while Motley kept the defense off balance with bursts through the middle of the line.

The final score was Cleveland 35, Philadelphia 10.

The Browns went on that season to win the NFL crown, defeating the Los Angeles Rams, 30–38, in the championship game, the one that Graham still considers his all-time favorite.

Despite two touchdown passes from

Graham to Jones and Lavelli, the Browns trailed, 28–20, early in the final quarter.

But with less than ten minutes to go, Graham hit Rex Baumgardner with a 14-yard pass, his fourth scoring aerial of the afternoon, and the Browns trailed by only a point, 28–27.

After two exchanges of punts, the Browns were down to their last chance with 1 minute 48 seconds to go and possession of the football on their own 32-yard line.

Graham, with all his receivers covered, ran for 14 yards and stepped out of bounds. He passed 15 yards to Baumgardner, who also stopped the clock by running out of bounds. Two more sideline passes, to Jones and Baumgardner, brought the ball to the Los Angeles 11 with 40 seconds to go.

Graham used one play to position the ball for Groza, sneaking for one yard himself after Baumgardner had told him his hands were cold and he feared he might fumble.

With twenty seconds showing on the clock, Groza carefully booted a 16-yard field goal that brought the frozen crowd of 29,751 to its feet, wildly cheering the new NFL champions.

No one doubted then that the Browns were the best professional football team in the world and that Graham was the game's preeminent quarterback. Against the Rams he had completed 22 of 33 passes for 298 yards and four touchdowns. Making pro football history, the Browns reached the title game for the next five years under Graham's guiding arm, and capped their star quarterback's career with championships in 1954 and 1955.

In 1954, they trounced the Detroit Lions, 56–10, as Graham ran for three touchdowns, passed for three, and handed off for the other two, in one of his greatest games. Following this game, Graham announced his retirement.

But when the Browns' quarterbacking situation became desperate in training camp the following season, Brown convinced Graham to return for one more season.

"It was tempting fate, I'll admit," said Otto after the 1955 season. "But we got away with it."

Get away with it they did, as Graham led the league in passing for the second time in three years.

Then, in his final game, he engineered a 38–14 triumph over the Rams by running for two scores and passing for two more. After the game, Brown called the 34-year-old Graham "the greatest quarterback ever to play in that spot."

"My second annual retirement from football," quipped Graham, "is a permanent one—positively, absolutely, and for keeps."

The game lost one of its finest natural passers.

"He is a pure passer," said Brown of his departing star. "He has a natural gift for throwing a pass that is straight, soft, and easy to catch. He seems to pull the string on the ball and set it down right over the receiver's head. This is the big thing for a T quarterback."

Graham once demonstrated his extraordinary accuracy by passing a football ten times in succession, from a distance of fifteen feet, through a wire coat hanger pulled into a diamond shape.

"This was nothing I deserved any medal for," he later explained. "I hadn't labored at it. It just turned out that I was able to do it."

Taking his natural passing ability for granted, Graham attributed his success to desire and hard work.

"To win in football, you have to give it everything you've got," he said. "At the same time, I don't believe you should ever

49ers pounce on Graham in 1946 game, but it's too late—he completed his pass.

An exhilarated Graham is interviewed after playing his last game and retiring with another NFL championship.

get mean or vicious about it.

"When we lost, it generally was because we played lousy football. And the answer usually would be that we didn't have the necessary desire. To win football games, you have to block and tackle as hard as you can."

Graham was born in Waukegan, Illinois, also famed as the home of Jack Benny, on December 6, 1921. Because his father was the director of instrumental music at the local high school, he learned to play the piano, violin, cornet, and French horn as a boy. But, with his natural athletic ability, he soon was spending more time at sports —all sports.

Although young Otto showed talent in football and track, basketball became his best sport. After a high school career which won him all-state honors, he went to Northwestern on a basketball scholarship.

In his freshman year he weighed only 160 pounds, and he attracted no immediate attention from the football coaches until they saw him passing in an intramural touch football game.

A cartilage operation on his knee, which had been wrenched playing softball (his only serious injury in sports), made it necessary for him to be inactive one year so as not to lose eligibility for either basketball or football.

As a sophomore, he began as an understudy to triple-threat Bill DeCorrevont, an Illinois schoolboy all-American. But soon Graham was the starter, and he led the team in scoring with eight touchdowns, as well as passing and punting. Operating from the tailback spot in the single wing in his three years at Northwestern, he became what his coach, Lynn ("Pappy") Waldorf, called "one of the greatest, if not the greatest, all-around backfield men I have ever had the privilege of coaching."

In his senior year, he was voted the most valuable player in the Big Ten, and won all-American recognition in both football and basketball.

While he was playing service football in the Navy Preflight Program, he was contacted by Paul Brown, who was already beginning to think of the team he planned to organize in Cleveland after the war.

In the spring of 1945, Brown signed Graham for a yearly salary of $7,500, but threw in a bonus of $200 a month for the duration of the war to lure Graham away from the Detroit Lions, who had drafted him in the NFL.

Before joining the Browns in 1946, Graham played professional basketball with the Rochester Royals of the National Basketball Association. Playing at forward with such gifted backcourt men as Bob Davies, Red Holzman, and Fuzzy Levane, Graham was a contributory force as the Royals won the league championship.

When he joined the Browns, he quickly made the adjustment as the T quarterback.

"I was lucky," he recalled later. "I didn't have an established quarterback in the NFL to go up against. We were all rookies. We all learned together. What helped me more than anything else was the fact that I was a good basketball player. The mechanics of quarterbacking are just the same as in basketball. The footwork and the pivoting are identical. You find a good basketball player, he's a good athlete."

In the first years of the AAC, Graham and the Browns introduced the sideline pass, an offensive move that revolutionized passing patterns. Mac Speedie or Dante Lavelli would run a standard zig-in, zig-out pattern, then suddenly head for the sideline where Graham would hit the receiver just before he ran out of bounds.

"It's a very tough pass to cover if you have a quarterback who can throw the football," said Graham. "The secret is to have the receiver come back. You tell a guy to make a 90-degree cut, but actually with momentum he's still going downfield. By making the receiver come back, he has the defender beaten by two steps. The defender is even blocked off by the receiver's body. I used to throw the football in relation to where the defensive man was, not where my man was.

"Even after a half-dozen years, I'd work with Speedie, Lavelli, and Dub Jones for hours after practice to keep sharp. It got so, if the receiver moved his fanny a certain way, I knew what he was going to do."

In his later years with Cleveland, the outspoken Graham was critical of Brown for sending in most of the plays by messenger guards.

"In a way, we have eleven coaches on the field. Various players will report to me on plays that might work. Paul Brown also will get that information, but my criticism of his system would be that he may be one or two plays behind what I myself would have called."

But Graham's criticism of Brown's play-calling system did not diminish his appreciation of Brown as a total coach.

"Paul was a great coach before I ever played for him," he said in his final year. "And he'll be a great coach after I'm gone."

Brown's appreciation of Graham has not diminished over the years, either. Now the head coach of the Cincinnati Bengals, he says simply, "Graham was the best."

All-America Conference

Year	Team	Games	Att.	Comp.	Pct.	Yards	TDs	Long	Int.	Pct. Int.	Avg. Gain
1946	Clev.	14	174	95	54.6	1834	17	t79	5	2.9	10.54
1947	Clev.	14	269	163	60.6	2753	25	t99	11	4.1	10.23
1948	Clev.	14	333	173	52.0	2713	25	t78	15	4.5	8.15
1949	Clev.	13	285	161	56.5	2785	19	t74	10	3.5	9.77
Totals 4 yrs.		55	1061	592	55.8	10,085	86	t99	41	3.9	9.51

National Football League

Year	Team	Games	Att.	Comp.	Pct.	Yards	TDs	Long	Int.	Pct. Int.	Avg. Gain
1950	Clev.	12	253	137	54.2	1943	14	31	20	7.9	7.68
1951	Clev.	12	265	147	55.5	2205	17	t81	16	6.0	8.32
1952	Clev.	12	364	181	49.7	2816	20	68	24	6.6	7.74
1953	Clev.	12	258	167	64.7	2722	11	70	9	3.5	10.55
1954	Clev.	12	240	142	59.2	2092	11	t64	17	7.1	8.72
1955	Clev.	12	185	98	53.0	1721	15	t61	8	4.3	9.30
Totals 6 yrs.		72	1565	872	55.7	13,499	88	t81	94	6.0	8.63

Zig-zags through Philadelphia's defenders for a 10-yard gain in debut as Steelers' quarterback in 1958 and sparks Pittsburgh to a 24-3 upset triumph.

Bobby Layne

Bobby Layne

by Lud Duroska

T he low point in Bobby Layne's football career arrived one September evening in 1958. The 31-year-old quarterback, who normally had the rollicking manner of a sailor on a weekend pass, was bitter and discouraged when he called his wife Carol in Lubbock, Texas, to discuss his future. As recently as the season before, he had been the toast of Detroit for his exploits as the Lions' field general. For eight years he had made the team a powerful contender, and in 1952 and 1953 he had led the Lions to league championships. But now the wolves were howling.

Personal misfortune had struck late in the 1957 season. The blond Texan, cajoling and driving his teammates in his husky drawl, was leading the Lions to another title. Then, in a game against the Cleveland Browns, Layne was blitzed and gang-tac-

Wide World
Layne dodges away from would-be Philadelphia tacklers in snow.

42

kled to the ground. He had to be carried off the field, his right leg fractured. His understudy, Tobin Rote, stepped in for the rest of the season. On crutches, Layne watched from the sidelines as the Lions walloped the Browns, 59–14, to win the NFL crown.

When the next summer rolled around, Layne was raring to go again. But his first competitive start was a disaster. Four of his passes were intercepted by the College All-Stars, who posted one of their infrequent victories, 35–19. But a greater blow to Layne followed. Coach George Wilson decided to divide the quarterbacking chores between Layne and Tobin Rote. This was particularly annoying to Layne, an outspoken advocate of the one-boss-on-the-field theory. He wanted to be in charge at all times, calling all the plays. Instead, he was on part-time duty, and the Lions lost their opening game. In the second game he played badly in a 13–13 tie against the Green Bay Packers. The fans began to boo. The press wondered in print whether he was too old to come back from such a devastating injury or had lost his passing skills. His confidence disappearing, Layne wondered if it was time to end his career.

"I seriously thought about retiring," he admitted later. That's when he called Carol to discuss his future as a quarterback. The couple agreed he would stay in Detroit for the time being and she would fly up the next day to help him through the crisis.

But the crisis ended suddenly. At the airport, meeting Carol, Bobby was paged for a phone call. The conversation was brief—he had been traded to the Pittsburgh Steelers for Earl Morrall and two draft choices. The abrupt parting from the Lions was a blow, but now he had a new challenge: to show everyone he wasn't washed up. It didn't matter that the Steelers were a dispirited, mediocre club; he was supposed to be a leader and he would lead them.

Happily, he would be reunited with his old coach, Buddy Parker. The two men understood and respected each other—they had worked well together while the Lions were climbing to the top. Parker had strongly indicated his confidence in Bobby Layne by making the trade.

Imbued with new determination, Layne couldn't wait to get to Pittsburgh. He left Detroit that night. Driving out to the Steelers' practice field the next morning with the publicity man, he was all business, learning the nicknames of his new teammates and their backgrounds.

Layne proved a revelation to them at the first workout. He moved in with the authority of the old pro, quickly establishing a rapport as he hustled his teammates through their assignments. He put into use what he had once advised:

"As a quarterback, you have to make the boys believe in you. Just the way you bark out the signals can tell them if you have confidence in the play you called. And they have to want to make it work. They have to be willing to put out an extra ten percent."

The Steelers proved willing. "You could almost see the transformation," one club official commented. "He made the players believe in themselves again—that they could be winners."

The Steelers had been badly trounced in their first two games. The Philadelphia Eagles were their next opponent and, naturally, Pittsburgh was the underdog. But Layne, with the team only six days, exhorted, goaded and commanded, and the Steelers produced a 24–3 upset.

John Nisby, a guard, typified the team's reaction to Layne. "He asks you to do something and you go out and break your neck to do it."

Layne and the Steelers couldn't overcome the superiority of their following two foes—the Cleveland Browns and the New York Giants—but they didn't lose again that season. They won six and tied one, and finished in third place in the Eastern Division for their best showing in years. Buddy Parker smiled in satisfaction. "Layne turned us into a football team," the coach declared. "He's the only guy who could have made so much difference so fast."

Layne also made a big personal difference to Jimmy Orr, a rookie end, that season. Always willing to stay after practice and to work with any receiver who wanted his help, he discovered an eager student in Orr.

As Parker explained, "Bobby showed him [Orr] how to handle his passes. He taught him new things about the pass patterns, and he picked out flaws during a game that we couldn't see from the sidelines."

As a result of the additional tutelage, Orr developed rapidly, and he earned league honors as rookie of the year, the first step toward a long and successful career as one of the better pass-catchers in the NFL.

Orr possessed the attributes that Layne appreciated. "He works hard and he's got guts," the old pro remarked. "One game he got clobbered and when I leaned over to find out if he was okay, he just looked up and said: 'Did I catch the ball?'

" 'You caught it,' I said.

" 'Good,' he said. 'I'll be back after one play.' He was back, too. That's the kind of player I like."

Robert Lawrence Layne was born on December 19, 1926, in Santa Anna, Texas. When he was six years old, his father died, and he was adopted by an aunt and uncle in Fort Worth. Later, the family moved to Dallas, where Bobby was enrolled at Highland Park High School. The boy became a dedicated competitor on the gridiron. As a freshman he played guard, and in his sophomore year he was switched to tail-back. The fellow he beat out for the starting position was a precocious freshman named Doak Walker, but the association began a long football friendship. Working together in the same backfield, the two players soon displayed the drive that separates champions from also-rans. After regular daily workouts, they remained on the field until dark, working on their passing and place-kicking skills.

In other seasons Bobby played baseball so well that he pitched the American Legion team to the state championship in 1943. Upon graduation from high school, he accepted a baseball scholarship to the University of Texas. "I wasn't even sure I wanted to play football in college," he recalls.

But that was a temporary feeling. Although he was outstanding as a college hurler—he never suffered a defeat at Texas —football soon became his first interest. After a fine freshman year as a tailback, he and Walker, who had just graduated from high school, enlisted in the merchant marine. World War II ended before they could be assigned to actual sea duty, however, and they were discharged in time for the football season.

Although he had planned to join Bobby at Texas, Doak was lured to Southern Methodist University. Within a week the two schoolboy chums were on opposing sides of the gridiron in a memorable game. SMU was leading, 7–6, and the two friendly competitors had been the whole show— Layne passing for a touchdown but missing the extra point, and Walker running for a score and kicking the conversion. Late in the final period, Doak piloted SMU downfield, attempting a pass into the end zone for the clinching six-pointer. But Bobby intercepted and ran the ball out to the 30 yard line. Layne passed the Longhorns 70 yards in three plays with less than two minutes left for the deciding touchdown.

Perils of being a quarterback—Cardinals' rusher knocks ball out of Layne's hand.

At the end of his junior year, when Bobby was getting all-American attention, two important events occurred. He married a coed, Carol Ann Krueger, and he was introduced to the T-formation by the new coach, Blair Cherry, who had taken over after Dana X. Bible retired. Bobby wasn't keen about changing to the T at first. "I don't feel like switching positions, now that I'm a senior in college," he said.

But after Cherry took Bobby and his bride to the Chicago Cardinals' training camp that summer to absorb the intricacies of the T, the new quarterback approached his task with his customary enthusiasm.

"Bobby never forgot for a moment that the purpose of the trip was to learn the T," Cherry remembered. "On the way home, we'd get out of the car when we stopped for gas. Bobby would get his wife around back of the car and have her serve as a center while he practiced the way he thought a T quarterback should play. Those service-station attendants probably thought we were off our rockers."

Bobby and the T clicked so well for Texas in his final year that the Longhorns won all their games except one. SMU and Bobby's old buddy, Doak Walker, spoiled a perfect season with a 14–13 defeat.

Now a bona fide all-American, Bobby could afford to be choosy about joining the pros. In 1948 the All-America Conference was still battling the National Football League for the best collegiate talent. Learning that the Steelers, then a single wing team, wanted him as their No. 1 draft pick, he boldly informed them that he wished to play for a T-formation club. Rather than lose him to the Baltimore Colts of the rival league, the Steelers drafted him and then traded Bobby to the Chicago Bears. He signed at handsome figures for those days—a bonus of $10,000 and a salary of $18,000.

But with the veteran Sid Luckman and

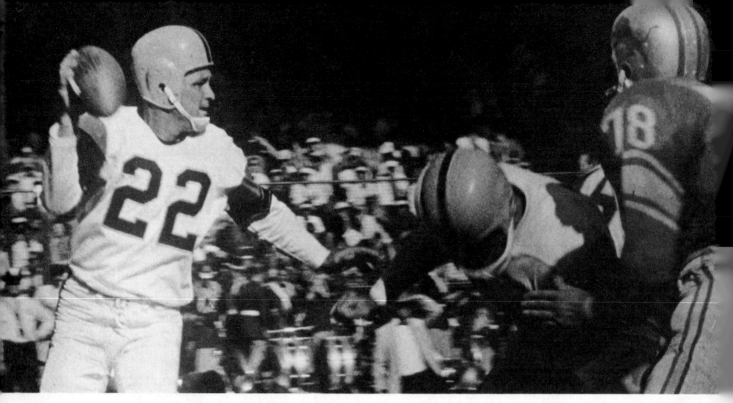

Holding ball aloft, Layne weighs his next move—pass or run?—as teammates block.

Johnny Lujack, the highly acclaimed Notre Dame star, on the team, Layne was relegated to third-string status and mostly rode the bench. He threw only 52 passes and completed 16. An unimpressed George Halas traded him in 1949 to the hapless New York Bulldogs. It proved a harrowing but educational year. The Bulldogs lost sixteen of eighteen games (including exhibitions), and Bobby's weight dropped from 205 pounds to 176 pounds. Nevertheless, Bobby Layne demonstrated that he had the courage and stamina to survive as a pro.

His luck turned when the Detroit Lions made a deal for him. Layne became their No. 1 quarterback, and he was reunited with Doak Walker. But the club was not happy with Coach Bo McMillin. The Lions had not been faring well under his strict rule. The players' resentments were made known to the Lions' management, who let McMillin go and hired Buddy Parker for the 1951 season.

Parker put Layne in complete charge on the field and the Lions started to roar. That season they were in title contention, missing out only on the last day of the season.

The following year the Lions brought a

world championship to Detroit for the first time since 1935. Layne blossomed into a running as well as a passing star and was accorded all-pro quarterback honors. Using the running options of the split-T, he gained more yardage—411—than any other Lion back except Bob Hoernschemeyer (475) and placed ninth among the league's rushing leaders. He also connected on 139 of 287 passes for 19 touchdowns and one yard short of the 2,000-yard mark.

On a brisk, sunny December afternoon in Cleveland, the Lions faced the redoubtable Browns, who were making their seventh straight appearance (with only one loss) in a league title contest. Blending the ground and air game cleverly, Layne directed the Lions' first thrust early in the second period, plunging over center from the Cleveland 2 for the first score. In the third quarter he handed off to Walker, who cut over right tackle and raced 67 yards for the clinching touchdown. Detroit won, 17–7.

Layne's finest moments came in the 1953 title rematch with the Browns. Before 54,-577 fans in Briggs Stadium, the Lions were on the short end of a 16–10 score with four minutes and ten seconds remaining in a game that had been sloppily played on a soft gridiron. Detroit had failed to score in the second half and some of the spectators were already heading for the exits when the Lions got the ball on their 20. But Layne, the confident and fiery competitor, said in the huddle:

"Just block a little bit, fellows, and ol' Bobby will pass you right to the championship."

Usually he threw to Dorne Dibble and Doak Walker, as the Browns were well aware. Layne crossed them up and threw twice to Jim Doran, a substitute little noticed by the Cleveland secondary. A defensive end, Doran was only playing on offense because Leon Hart had been injured earlier in the game. A third pass to Cloyce Box advanced Detroit to the Browns' 48. Switching tactics, Layne handed off to Hoernschemeyer on one running play and carried the ball himself on the next, driving for a first down on the Cleveland 33. Then he faked a handoff and stepped back in the pocket. Doran ran

down the sideline and got behind Warren Lahr, the Browns' cornerback. Layne's throw was right on the mark, and Doran grabbed the ball in the end zone to tie the score. The Lions' leader had made good on his promise—he had piloted the team 80 yards in two minutes! With Layne holding, Walker booted the winning conversion, and the Lions were champions again.

Layne survived as a pro for fifteen years —through good seasons and bad—and he always gave that 110 percent. He surpassed the great Sammy Baugh's record for total passes attempted and completed, for total yardage, and for touchdown passes.

His old schoolboy chum remembers his special qualities. "Bobby never lost a game. Time just ran out," said Doak Walker. "Nobody hated to lose more than Bobby. He never was erratic, always cool. It didn't matter if we were ahead by 20 points or behind by 20, he was the same. He ran the team. Nobody else could do it the way he did."

Year	Team	Games	Att.	Comp.	Pct.	Yards	TDs	Long	Int.	Pct. Int.	Avg. Gain
1948	Chi.B.	11	52	16	30.8	232	3	35	2	3.8	4.46
1949	N.Y.B.	12	299	155	51.8	1796	9	69	18	6.0	6.01
1950	Det.	12	336	152	45.2	2323	16	t82	18	5.4	6.91
1951	Det.	12	332	152	45.8	2403	26	63	23	6.9	7.24
1952	Det.	12	287	139	48.4	1999	19	t77	20	7.0	6.97
1953	Det.	12	273	125	45.8	2088	16	t97	21	7.7	7.65
1954	Det.	12	246	135	54.9	1818	14	55	12	4.9	7.39
1955	Det.	12	270	143	53.0	1830	11	t77	17	6.3	6.78
1956	Det.	12	244	129	52.9	1909	9	70	17	7.0	7.82
1957	Det.	11	179	87	48.6	1169	6	t65	12	6.7	6.53
1958	Det.-Pitt.	12	294	145	49.3	2510	14	t78	12	4.1	8.54
1959	Pitt.	12	297	142	47.8	1986	20	48	21	7.1	6.69
1960	Pitt.	12	209	103	49.3	1814	13	70	17	8.1	8.68
1961	Pitt.	8	149	75	50.3	1205	11	53	16	10.7	8.09
1962	Pitt.	13	233	116	49.8	1686	9	62	17	7.3	7.24
Totals 15 yrs.		175	3700	1814	49.0	26,768	196	t97	243	6.6	7.23

Slips ball to Jon Arnett on scoring play as Rams open path against 49ers.

NormVanBrocklin

Norm Van Brocklin

by Murray Chass

It was the morning of December 26, 1960, and the scene was the home team's locker room at Franklin Field in Philadelphia. The Eagles were to play the Green Bay Packers for the National Football League championship in a few hours, and the players were starting to arrive.

Solemnly, they entered the locker room, ready to dress and prepare for the game as quietly as if they were in church. But Norm Van Brocklin wouldn't let them stay that way for long. Sitting cross-legged atop a trunk at the entrance to the clubhouse, the Philadelphia quarterback had a light and cheery word for everyone, words that broke the tension each Eagle felt.

A laugher and a joker, Van Brocklin soon had his teammates laughing and jok-

UPI
Van Brocklin throws for long gainer, with Ted Dean by his side, in 17-13 title victory against Green Bay Packers in 1960.

ing, and the loose and carefree atmosphere prevailed for the rest of the day as the Eagles went out and won a championship that no one had expected them to win.

But winning the title was no surprise to the people who knew Van Brocklin best, for often they had seen "The Dutchman" pull off the unexpected. He did it in various ways—with his unerring passing, with his wily play-calling, and with his fiery leadership. If a situation called for a pinpoint pass at the sideline forty yards away, Van Brocklin could toss it. If the moment begged for a play that would surprise the opposition, Van Brocklin could call it. If a harsh taunt was necessary to fire up a player, Van Brocklin could deliver it.

Nothing about his behavior surprised his teammates. "I saw him lose his composure, but there usually was a reason for it," recalled Don Burroughs, an Eagle defensive back. "With him, there was no substitute for winning. He felt that we were getting paid to play right and win."

"As well as I knew him off the field," added another Eagle defensive back, Tom Brookshier, "any time he thought I wasn't playing right he'd bawl the hell out of me. That's what some people didn't understand about him—the difference between on the field and off it."

On the field, Van Brocklin was concerned with only one thing—winning. He dedicated himself to that goal, and he expected everyone else on his team to do the same. It was an attitude that led to a glittering twelve-year career in which "The Dutchman" completed more than half his passes—1,553 of 2,895, or 53.6 percent —threw for 23,611 yards and 173 touchdowns, and became the first quarterback to lead two different teams to championships.

Three times Van Brocklin won the National Football League passing title and twice he sparked his team to the NFL championship—once with Los Angeles

and once with Philadelphia. Furthermore, he was selected to play in the All-Star game in nine of his twelve seasons.

In spite of these accomplishments, there were football people who considered Van Brocklin something less than a complete football player.

"Van Brocklin can throw, period," George Halas of the Chicago Bears once said. "In the full sense of the word, he is not a professional player." Of course, all Van Brocklin had done that day to Halas' Bears was forge a 40–24 victory on 308 yards passing, including touchdown tosses of 84, 61, 56, and 20 yards!

In another bitter comment, a San Francisco 49er coach said, "Van Brocklin is the all-time freak. If the game hadn't turned pass-happy, he wouldn't be able to play with the semi-pros. All he has is an arm. He runs like a girl with her girdle slipping. He couldn't block a baby or play any other position. Just blow hard and he falls down."

Saying that all Van Brocklin could do was pass is like saying that all Bob Hope can do is tell jokes or that all Rembrandt could do was paint. There are, of course, football purists who believe a player should be able to do everything on a football field. But if a tackle isn't expected to be able to throw a 50-yard pass, why should a quarterback be expected to block a 260-pound defensive tackle?

Indeed, Van Brocklin was almost strictly a passer (he also punted for twelve years, leading the league twice). But he was a great passer and he could do things with the football that many other quarterbacks couldn't do. There was the time, for instance, when the Eagles were playing a heavily favored New York Giant team. Philadelphia had the ball at its nine-yard line and definitely needed something that would instill a spark into its lagging forces.

Van Brocklin quickly glanced at the

Giant defense and stepped into the huddle. Pointing to Tommy McDonald, the team's fastest receiver, he said, "Go down the right sideline, Tommy, and just run. I don't know where the ball will hit you, but it will."

With another quarterback, McDonald might have been skeptical. But when it was Van Brocklin giving the orders, McDonald simply listened and did what he was told. The ball was snapped, McDonald took off down the sideline and Van Brocklin backpedaled into the end zone. Waiting as long as he possibly could, until the Giant linemen were approaching menacingly, the quarterback uncorked a tremendous throw, sailing the ball 65 yards to the Giant 40 where McDonald plucked it out of the air and kept going until he reached the other end zone for a 91-yard touchdown that catapulted the Eagles to a 27–24 victory.

Another time, on the practice field, Van Brocklin displayed his uncanny ability to perform tricks with the football. He was with Los Angeles at the time, and a teammate one day decided to see how accurate the quarterback could be as a passer.

"Dutchman," said the teammate, "throw a pass and let it stop on the ground and then see how close you can come to hitting the ball. You can have ten chances to hit it."

"What if I hit it?" Van Brocklin asked.

"I'll give you a Coke for every hit," the teammate replied.

Taking the ball, Van Brocklin threw a pass that landed about 35 yards away. Then, taking his ten throws, Van Brocklin hit the first ball an incredible six times.

"That'll be six Cokes," he told his friend.

"I don't believe it," the player said, his mouth more than a little bit open.

Contrary to what it might seem, Norman Van Brocklin did not enter the world throwing 35-yard strikes with a football. Born in Eagle Butte, South Dakota, on March 15, 1926, Norm was the eighth of nine children in the farming Van Brocklin family. The family remained in South Dakota during the early years of Norm's childhood, and then moved to Walnut Creek, California, at which time "those awful winds of the early thirties blew all the dirt off our farm and my father didn't want to starve."

At Acalanes High School in Walnut Creek, Van Brocklin became a standout in football, baseball, and basketball, and acquired the nickname "Stubby," which would later be inappropriate for his six-foot-two-inch, 205-pound frame.

Following high school, Van Brocklin couldn't take advantage of his athletic ability immediately—he was considered a potential major-league pitcher at the time —because World War II was in progress, and he joined the Navy.

The first year after his discharge wasn't much more promising, as far as a professional sports career was concerned. Attending the University of Oregon under the GI Bill of Rights, Van Brocklin played varsity football in his first year (freshmen were then eligible), but during his total playing time of eleven minutes, he threw only nine passes, completing none and having three intercepted.

Then came the break Van Brocklin needed. A slow runner, freshman Van Brocklin hadn't fit into Coach Tex Oliver's single wing formation. But before Norm's sophomore year, Jim Aiken replaced Oliver as coach and installed the T-formation. Looking for a quarterback to operate the new attack, Aiken quickly found his man in Van Brocklin.

But Aiken's first order to his quarterback had nothing to do with passing or play-calling. Grabbing Norm's right hand, the coach smelled his nicotine-stained fin-

Van Brocklin looking to pass before 49er tackles him.

gers and ordered, "No more smoking."

"He scared me half to death," Van Brocklin said some years later. "I had to quit smoking."

He also started passing, and did it so well that he led the Pacific Coast Conference in passing for two seasons, and in 1948 led Oregon to nine victories in ten games and an appearance in the Cotton Bowl.

Van Brocklin had another year of varsity eligibility remaining, but passed it up to play pro ball. No one knew it at the time, but Norm had taken enough summer courses to earn the required number of credits to graduate in three years instead of four.

While at Oregon, he married Gloria Schiewe, who had been his lab instructor in a biology course, and he felt he would be better off earning money as a pro than playing another year in college. So he tipped off the Rams as to his availability in the draft, and the Rams picked him, much to the surprise of the rest of the teams in the NFL, not to mention his college coach.

As a rookie, Van Brocklin found himself a third-stringer behind Bob Waterfield and Jim Hardy. Still, he got into eight games, although it wasn't until the final game of the season, when the Rams needed a victory over the Washington Redskins to clinch the division title, that Norm got his big chance. And then he almost blew it.

Entering the game early in the first quarter, Van Brocklin fumbled and the Redskins turned the mistake into a touchdown. "I thought I was a goner," Norm said. But he wasn't. Clark Shaughnessy, the Ram coach, walked over to him and said, "Don't let that trouble you, son. I'm putting you right back in."

Buoyed by the coach's confidence in him, Van Brocklin responded by firing four touchdown passes and leading the Rams to a 53–27 decision and into the first of his five championship games.

Joe Stydahar replaced Shaughnessy as coach for the 1950 season, and decided to split the quarterbacking evenly between Waterfield and Van Brocklin. Not only did the Rams win the Western Division title again, but Van Brocklin also led the NFL in passing and powered the Rams to a share of a record that may never be equaled again.

Playing against the Detroit Lions on October 29, 1950, the Rams exploded for 41 points in the third quarter, with four of the touchdowns coming on passes from Van Brocklin—31 yards to Elroy ("Crazy Legs") Hirsch, 43 to Glenn Davis, 30 to Tom Fears, and 42 to Bob Boyd.

The following season, Van Brocklin erupted again for a record-shattering performance. In a game against the New York Yankees on September 28, 1951, Norm amassed 554 yards in the air for another mark that may never be eclipsed.

Despite such a prolific effort, all was not well between coach Stydahar and quarterback Van Brocklin that season. Their differences of opinion reached the breaking point in the final regular-season game against Green Bay, when Van Brocklin ignored a running play sent in by the coach and passed instead.

An angry Stydahar pulled Van Brocklin from the game and sent in Bob Waterfield, who promptly accumulated enough passing statistics to beat out his teammate for the league passing title.

Van Brocklin was still on the bench when the Rams met the Cleveland Browns for the NFL title. Waterfield played most of the game, but with the score tied, 17–17, in the fourth quarter, Van Brocklin took over and combined with Tom Fears on a 73-yard touchdown pass that ended the Browns' domination of the NFL.

After another season, the Rams' quarterback problems ended because Waterfield retired, leaving the job to Van Brocklin. But Van Brocklin didn't have much time to enjoy his status as the team's un-challenged No. 1 quarterback.

The first problem cropped up in the 1955 title game against Cleveland, when Van Brocklin had six passes intercepted, and the Rams lost, 38–14. "It was the worst game I ever played," he acknowledged. The following season, Sid Gillman, who had replaced Stydahar as coach for 1955, decided to split the duties between Van Brocklin and Billy Wade, the team's top draft pick in 1954.

The plan didn't work very well, though, so Gillman gave the job back to Van Brocklin in 1957. But relations between the player and the coach continued to be strained, because Gillman insisted on calling the plays from the sidelines and Van Brocklin strongly resented it.

"You give the quarterback a ready list and feed him information," Norm argued, "but he's the only one who can get the actual feel of the play on the field. The quarterback has to be the leader."

Having had enough of being something less than the No. 1 quarterback and offensive leader, Van Brocklin asked to be traded following the 1957 season. He got his wish—although he wound up with the Eagles, the one team he had specifically asked Pete Rozelle, then the Los Angeles general manager, *not* to send him to.

"Buck Shaw, the Philadelphia coach, called me and said he got me in a trade," Van Brocklin related. "But I told him I wasn't going to report. Then I called Rozelle and chewed him out real good for double-crossing me."

Norm, however, learned later that Bert Bell, the NFL commissioner, had persuaded Rozelle to let the quarterback go to Philadelphia because the Eagles were an ailing franchise and needed help. As good as Van Brocklin was, he couldn't help much in 1958, and the Eagles won only two games.

But then the patient started improving, and in 1960 the doctor led the Eagles to the Eastern Division title. The Eagles really weren't a team of championship caliber, as seemed obvious from their opening-game 41–24 loss to Cleveland. But Van Brocklin rallied them to victories in their next nine games, sparking comebacks during the second half in five of those contests.

"Nobody ever played quarterback like Van Brocklin played it for the Eagles in 1960," says Alex Karras, the Detroit Lions' tackle who has had some experience with quarterbacks.

The climax of that season came in the championship contest against Green Bay, a game played on a muddy surface at Franklin Field in Philadelphia. Just as in the title game in 1951, Van Brocklin found his team needing a score in the final quarter. This time, though, the Eagles trailed, 13–10.

Ted Dean got Philadelphia going with a 58-yard kickoff return to the Packer 39-yard line, and Van Brocklin took over from there with his masterful play-calling. The Packers, expecting a long pass in an attempt for a quick touchdown, dropped back, but Van Brocklin sent Dean off tackle and then Billy Barnes through the middle. He used his running backs in this manner until the Eagles moved the ball inside the 20.

Then, when the Packers finally moved in to choke off the successful running attack, Van Brocklin fired a quick pass to Barnes over the middle for 13 yards. The Eagles had the ball at the 5 now and the Packers felt another pass coming. But the quarterback sent Dean around end, the rookie reached the end zone, and the Eagles won the championship, 17–13.

Following that unbelievably successful season, Van Brocklin did something few professional athletes can or will do—he retired on top. Deciding he had thrown enough passes, goaded enough teammates, snarled at enough opposing linemen, and argued with enough coaches, he became a coach himself. His career was placed in proper perspective some years later, when he was elected to two Halls of Fame, the college and the pro.

Sid Gillman, one of the coaches with whom he argued, also helped put Van Brocklin's ability in the proper focus. "Van Brocklin's lack of speed is a terrible disadvantage in this age of running and passing quarterbacks," Gillman said at the height of Van Brocklin's tenure with the Rams. "But he still has the one big thing that pays off in football—he throws the ball straight. There is no defense against a quarterback who can throw straight. That's Van's strong suit."

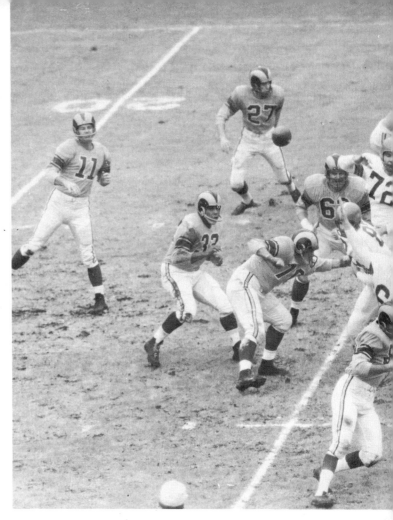

Van Brocklin pitches a pass for Rams against Cleveland in 1955 title game.

Year	Team	Games	Att.	Comp.	Pct.	Yards	TDs	Long	Int.	Pct. Int.	Avg. Gain
1949	L.A.	8	58	32	55.2	601	6	t51	2	3.4	10.36
1950	L.A.	12	233	127	54.5	2061	18	58	14	6.0	8.85
1951	L.A.	12	194	100	51.5	1725	13	t81	11	5.7	8.89
1952	L.A.	12	205	113	55.1	1736	14	t84	17	8.3	8.47
1953	L.A.	12	286	156	54.5	2393	19	t70	14	4.9	8.37
1954	L.A.	12	260	139	53.5	2637	13	t80	21	8.1	10.14
1955	L.A.	12	272	144	52.9	1890	8	t74	15	5.5	6.95
1956	L.A.	12	124	68	54.8	966	7	t58	12	9.7	7.79
1957	L.A.	12	265	132	49.8	2105	20	t70	21	7.9	7.94
1958	Phil.	12	374	198	52.9	2409	15	t91	20	5.3	6.44
1959	Phil.	12	340	191	56.2	2617	16	71	14	4.1	7.70
1960	Phil.	12	284	153	53.9	2471	24	t64	17	6.0	8.70
Totals 12 yrs.		**140**	**2895**	**1553**	**53.6**	**23,611**	**173**	**t91**	**178**	**6.1**	**8.16**

Under pressure, he throws high over Colt defender in 1958 title game.

Charley Conerly

Charley Conerly

by Lud Duroska

If ever an athlete lived up to Rudyard Kipling's definition of a man—to meet those two imposters, triumph and disaster, and treat them the same—it was Charley Conerly.

Whether it was the harrowing Sundays of the early 1950's, when he was the battered target of rushers as he waited in vain for glue-footed receivers to break into the clear, or whether it was the pleasurable Sundays later in the decade when he was surrounded by more capable teammates and was leading the New York Giants to title glory, it was the same Conerly—taciturn and uncomplaining in defeat, taciturn and unassuming in victory.

The quiet man from Mississippi knew well how fickle fate—and the fans—could be, and he was not deluded by either. He knew his own worth, and his demeanor and

UPI
Conerly tosses downfield as Packers' Tom Bettis follows ball.

Conerly gives ball to Webster . . . he hands off to Gifford . . .   Gifford slants over right guard . . .

character earned him the respect and admiration of his teammates. Other quarterbacks might employ the lash of the tongue,
but Conerly achieved results without bom-
bast or temper. In his time he was as good
a quarterback as there was in the National
Football League.

Kyle Rote, on Giant teams with Conerly
for eleven seasons, described him this way:

"His quiet confidence commanded respect. He never yelled or berated anyone
in the huddle. But there was always a
strength and determination in his manner
that made us believe in him."

In the record books Conerly's most fruit-
ful years were from 1956 to 1959, when he
guided the Giants to three division titles
and one world championship. And, in his
final days in 1961, as the oldest competitor
in the NFL at the age of 41, the gray-haired
passer celebrated his last hurrah in the un-
accustomed role of relief man by rallying
the Giants to two crucial triumphs that
helped them enter another championship
game.

It was during the 1959 season, his finest,
that Charley Conerly Day was held at
Yankee Stadium on Sunday, November 29.
The team's opponent that day was the
Washington Redskins, whose witty press

agent, Dick McCann, quipped: "It's only
fitting. The Redskins have been giving
Conerly 'days' ever since he has been in
the league." McCann was referring to the
fact that Charley so frequently enjoyed
stellar afternoons against the Redskins.
Ironically, he had been a Washington draft
choice, but he never did wear the Redskin
uniform.

On that blustery, sunny afternoon, in
pre-game ceremonies, 60,982 fans in the
stands applauded as Charley and his wife
Perian stood near the Giants' bench and
received a wide range of gifts. Typically,
he made his speech brief: "I want to thank
you all for sticking with me."

Then he went out on the field and ex-
pressed his appreciation more eloquently
by overcoming the traditional jinx of the
athlete who performs poorly on his own
'day.' Despite a sore right ankle, he deftly
directed the Giants' attack, and he threw
for three touchdowns. Twice he connected
with his split end, Bob Schnelker, for
scores from 7 and 34 yards out, and a
third time to Rote, a short toss into the end
zone from the 2, after a sustained march,
as New York rolled over the Redskins, 45–
14.

The following Sunday Conerly put on

nd then laterals to Conerly . . .   with Browns' Gain (70) in pursuit . . .   and scores despite Wren's tackle in 1958 playoff razzle-dazzler.

another virtuoso performance as the Giants demolished the Cleveland Browns, 48–7, and wrapped up the Eastern Division crown. By season's end he had 113 completions in 194 attempts for 1,706 yards and 14 touchdowns and, most remarkably, only four interceptions, all of which brought him his first NFL passing title. In addition, his fellow pros voted him the league's most valuable player, for which he earned the Jim Thorpe Trophy.

But he had paid his dues for this latter-day success. Only six years before he had been booed at the Polo Grounds as the scapegoat for hapless Giant teams. The crowd hung out banners reading: "Good-bye, Charley," and "Back to the Farm, Conerly." He was the victim of what Norm Van Brocklin called the "look-out" blocker, meaning a lineman who failed to stop his man and hollered, "Look out!" back at the quarterback.

The abuse rained on Conerly was not confined merely to his appearances on the gridiron. He was taunted even when he attended sporting events at Madison Square Garden.

"Some years it was so bad," he recalled, "that my wife and I just wouldn't go out evenings. I'd be recognized, and it didn't

matter to me so much what they said, but I didn't want my wife embarrassed."

Conerly first exhibited the toughness that enabled him to survive those weekly batterings when he was a combat Marine in World War II. Shortly after enrolling at the University of Mississippi, he enlisted in the Marines. As a corporal, he took part in the invasion of the Pacific island of Guam during the summer of 1942. Once, while on patrol, he had his carbine shot out of his hands by a Japanese sniper. Years later, talking about the heavy and bloody fighting in the jungle, he would only say, "It was kinda hot for a while."

The ex-Marine became an old-fashioned triple-threat when he returned to the Mississippi campus. He ran, passed, and punted as a single-wing tailback. In 1947 he won the National Collegiate Athletic Association passing title with 133 completions in 233 attempts for 1,567 yards and 18 touchdowns. His brilliant record made him an all-American, and he was coveted by the Giants in 1948.

But George Preston Marshall, owner of the Redskins, had drafted Conerly in 1945 (he was eligible for the draft because that was his original graduating class). The Giants tried to negotiate for Conerly, but

Marshall wouldn't part with him at first. Then the Redskins' owner drew the bonus pick out of the hat, which entitled him to first choice and he chose Harry Gilmer, the Alabama all-American passer.

In Marshall's eyes, that made Conerly expendable, and the Giants were able to get him for Howie Livingston, a halfback, and Pete Stout, a fullback, in a trade that proved a bargain, indeed. So Charley never did get to the Redskins' camp.

With the Giants in 1948, the Ole Miss graduate had as fine a first season as any great NFL passer ever had. He moved easily into Coach Steve Owen's A-Formation (which was comfortable for him because it was similar to the single wing) and compiled a dazzling set of statistics: 162 completions in 299 attempts for 1,175 yards and 22 touchdowns, all of which earned him rookie-of-the-year honors. Playing against the Pittsburgh Steelers late that season, he completed 36 passes, setting a pro-football record that stood for fourteen years.

He had a physically rough introduction to the pros. He was knocked out in the first two games, losing a tooth in the first and suffering a depressed fracture of the cheekbone in the second. But he took those injuries in stride, just as he took the broken bones and concussions that came later.

The following year the Giants' high command decided to change over to the T-formation. Allie Sherman, a bright second-string Eagles' quarterback from Brooklyn College, was hired to tutor Charley in the techniques of the T. Conerly wondered why the offensive system, which had worked well, was being changed. But, true to his nature, he offered no objections. He diligently practiced the pivots, the handoffs, and the pass drops. The transition required more than a season. In the meantime, the abilities of the rest of the Giant players declined.

Conerly managed to guide the Giants into a first-place tie with the Cleveland Browns in 1950. But they lost the playoff game when a last-minute scoring pass was nullified by a penalty.

The bleak Sundays of 1951, 1952, and 1953 followed. Conerly was constantly booed and jeered for the team's failings. Burdened by weak pass protection and slow receivers, he took many a beating. Since he waited until the last possible second to try to get the pass off, he left himself open to bone-jolting tackles by 260-pound behemoths. It made him more grim, but he never complained, and his teammates and opponents admired him for his quiet courage.

During one season he concealed from Coach Owen a shoulder injury that made throwing short passes extremely painful and long ones nearly impossible. Not until the final game did Owen learn of the injury.

"Why didn't you tell me?" asked the coach angrily.

"I had to stay in there," said Charley. "I was the only quarterback you had."

The club staggered through its worst season in 1953, winning three and losing nine. That winter, back in Mississippi, Conerly was on the verge of retiring, feeling he had taken enough punishment. By then a new coaching staff had taken over, with Jim Lee Howell as the head coach, Vince Lombardi in charge of the offense, and Tom Landry in charge of the defense. When the Giants heard about Conerly's retirement plans, Howell hustled down to Mississippi to talk to him. The quarterback was vital to his plans for the next season, and he convinced Charley to return by promising him better support.

Howell kept his word. The rebuilding process began in 1954. The Giants' coaches developed standout blockers such as Rosey Brown, Bill Austin, Ray Wietecha and Jack Stroud. They bolstered the receiving corps, which already had Rote, with Frank Gifford and Bob Schnelker. And they im-

Conerly remembers No. 1 rule—keep opponent from forcing a fumble.

UPI

Conerly spilled hard by Colts' Big Daddy Lipscomb in 1959 title game.

proved the running game with Alex Webster, Mel Triplett and the versatile Gifford.

It all clicked in 1956 as the Giants swept to the Eastern Division title and then routed the Chicago Bears, 47–7, for the NFL championship at Yankee Stadium. Conerly was a masterful field general in the 20-degree weather, throwing for two touchdowns and steering a hard-driving ground attack that overwhelmed the Bears on the ice-hard field. Charley received a standing ovation after the game, which must have given him tremendous satisfaction, but he displayed no emotion. He had done his job—and that was what he was being paid for.

Conerly and the Giants continued to be successful. But another world title eluded them in the famous sudden-death game with the Baltimore Colts in 1958 and again in

the title rematch with the Colts in 1959.

Through good and bad years Conerly mastered a very useful technique—the knack of throwing the ball away without incurring a penalty. No NFL quarterback was more adept at this than the Giants' star. Instead of being tackled for a large loss when a receiver was not open, Charley would toss the ball close enough to one of his receivers so that he appeared to be trying for a completion. At the same time, he made sure no defender had a chance to intercept (and he had an unusually low total of interceptions). During Conerly's career no official ever penalized him for intentionally grounding the ball.

The Giants were thwarted in their bid for a third consecutive division title in 1960, when they played the Eagles in the deciding game. Trailing, 17–10, Conerly had the Giants on the march in the closing minutes. He hit Gifford with a long pass deep into Philadelphia territory. But as Gifford turned to run, Chuck Bednarik, the hard-nosed Eagles' linebacker, delivered a "blind-side" tackle that jarred the ball loose. The collision was so violent that the Giant halfback sustained a severe concussion, forcing him to retire for a season. The Eagles recovered the fumble and the Giants' title hopes went down the drain.

As it must for all quarterbacks, the final season arrived for Conerly in 1961. Battle wounds and advancing age (41 years) had taken their toll. Charley was relegated to the bench in favor of the newly arrived Y. A. Tittle, who was five years younger. But the old pro still came to the rescue when needed.

After an opening loss, the Giants went on a winning streak. They were seeking their fifth victory of the season against the Los Angeles Rams before 63,053 fans at Yankee Stadium. Tittle had led the club to a 10–0 half-time lead, but the Rams had rallied and gone ahead, 14–10, in the second half. Tittle had suddenly lost his touch, so Allie Sherman turned to Conerly. The gray-haired warrior left the bench and fired up the Giants. During a 2-minute-3-second span in the fourth period, he led them on two scoring drives, capping one with a 10-yard pass to Kyle Rote and the other with a 37-yarder to speedy Del Shofner. He even fooled the Rams by calling his own number. He ran off tackle to gain a key first down on the Los Angeles 10 and set up the go-ahead score to Rote.

Conerly played the hero for the last time in the next-to-last game of the season. The Giants and Eagles were tied for first place again as they met on a foggy, rainy day at Franklin Field, Philadelphia, with the division crown at stake. The Eagles' defenses had been giving Tittle problems, so Conerly was sent in during the second period with Philadelphia ahead, 10–7. He struck quickly with a 35-yard touchdown pass to Joe Walton. Sherman kept him in the game in the second half and Charley collaborated with Shofner on a 26-yard completion to make the score 21–10. But the Eagles rallied and made it 21–17. Then Conerly drove the Giants down the field for the clinching touchdown, throwing to Shofner in the end zone from 11 yards out. A late Philadelphia tally did not prevent the Giants from winning, 28–24.

The Giants opposed the Packers in frigid Green Bay, Wisconsin, for league honors, but they were shut out, 37–0. Conerly's pinch-hitting could not pierce the Packers' armor. Two months later, Charley Conerly officially announced his retirement. At a farewell party for him in a New York restaurant, he responded to all the praise and accolades in his usual manner and set another record—a farewell speech which lasted less than fifteen seconds!

Year	Team	Games	Att.	Comp.	Pct.	Yards	TDs	Long	Int.	Pct. Int.	Avg. Gain
1948	N.Y.G.	12	299	162	54.2	2175	22	t65	13	4.3	7.27
1949	N.Y.G.	12	305	152	49.8	2138	17	t85	20	6.6	7.01
1950	N.Y.G.	11	132	56	42.4	1000	8	61	7	5.3	7.58
1951	N.Y.G.	12	189	93	49.2	1277	10	t69	22	11.6	6.76
1952	N.Y.G.	11	169	82	48.5	1090	13	t70	10	5.9	6.45
1953	N.Y.G.	12	303	143	47.2	1711	13	t60	25	8.3	5.65
1954	N.Y.G.	10	210	103	49.0	1439	17	t68	11	5.2	6.85
1955	N.Y.G.	12	202	98	48.5	2310	13	t71	13	6.4	11.44
1956	N.Y.G.	12	174	90	51.7	1143	10	48	7	4.0	6.57
1957	N.Y.G.	12	232	128	55.2	1712	11	70	11	4.7	7.38
1958	N.Y.G.	10	184	88	47.8	1199	10	44	9	4.9	6.52
1959	N.Y.G.	10	194	113	58.2	1706	14	t77	4	2.1	8.79
1960	N.Y.G.	12	134	66	49.3	954	8	70	7	5.2	7.12
1961	N.Y.G.	13	106	44	41.5	634	7	t37	8	7.5	5.98
Totals 14 yrs.		161	2833	1418	50.1	20,488	173	t85	167	5.9	7.23

Grips dry ball as Greg Larson (53) and Bookie Bolin (63) block in mud.

Y.A. Tittle

Y.A.Tittle
by Parton Keese

Thirty-eight years old, bald and jug-eared, even in his prime Y. A. Tittle looked more like a businessman than the player that Allie Sherman, his coach with the New York Giants, called "the greatest passer of our time."

The 6-foot, 195-pound Tittle, who wore old-fashioned high-topped shoes on the field and perused stock market tables through bifocals off the field, was living proof that appearances can be deceptive. In his seventeen-year career, Tittle was named the most valuable player in the NFL three times (1957, 1961, and 1963) and established a carload of passing records.

At one time he held the record for most touchdown passes in a career (212), most completions (2,118), and most yards gained (28,339). He still shares in records for most touchdown passes in a season

Bill Glass of Cleveland makes long stretch to tackle Tittle, but ball is already traveling to receiver.

(36) and most touchdown passes in a game (7).

But even in his most successful years with the Giants, Tittle's shy, taciturn ways and his disarming appearance proved an excellent disguise. Once, in 1962, following a group of Giant players onto an airplane, Tittle was stopped by the stewardess who said, "I'm sorry, sir. This flight is for football players only."

Tittle, not the least bit angered, looked up and said modestly, "But I *am* a football player."

In a football game, however, there was no mistaking Tittle's greatness. His talents as a passer were complemented by a tremendous enthusiasm. Many a fan may remember seeing Y. A. slam his helmet to the ground, disgusted either with himself or with a teammate he felt had not performed to the best of his ability.

To Tittle, however, football meant just one thing: passing. "Put the ball in the air" was a credo he had carried with him since early boyhood, when his idol was Sammy Baugh. Yelberton Abraham Tittle, Jr. was born in Marshall, Texas, on October 24, 1926, the son of a postman. Y. A. (as he preferred to call himself) learned to overcome the handicap of his name in much the same way as he learned to overcome the single wing, the popular formation of his very early days, which stressed running with the football, not passing.

The T-formation came into Tittle's life early in his Louisiana State University days, and he quickly gained a reputation as a hot-passing T quarterback. Drafted by the Cleveland Browns of the new All-America Conference, Tittle was immediately transferred to the Baltimore Colts, who needed a quarterback badly.

At his first pro game, he sat on the bench watching his team losing an exhibition contest to the Los Angeles Dons.

"If they don't get me in there soon, we're going to lose this thing," Tittle said to a player next to him. A few minutes later, Tittle repeated his remark. "I tell you," he said, "Isbell [Cecil Isbell, coach of the Colts] is going to blow this thing unless he puts me in there."

Whether Isbell heard Tittle or not, he waved him into the game. With only a few minutes left and the Colts trailing, 19–7, Tittle passed for a touchdown. After the Colt defense contained the Dons, Tittle again drove down the field, calling time-outs and throwing sideline passes to stop the clock.

As it was, time ran out before Tittle could lead his team in for the winning score, but his remarks on the bench and his performance in the game gained for Y. A. a reputation for self-confidence.

Isbell decided to open the season with Tittle, an untried rookie, as his quarterback. So what did Y. A. do? He set four AAC passing records in beating the New York Yankees, 45–28.

Another reputation haunted Tittle throughout his career, however. Scoffers said, "Tittle can't win the big ones," referring to the fact that Tittle never played with a team that won the league championship.

Injuries were one reason. Though Tittle was brittle, he managed to surmount most of his maladies during the ten years he played with the San Francisco 49ers and again during his three years with the Giants.

Tittle had a great career with the 49ers. As their quarterback, from 1952 to 1960, he guided the team to second place three times, and they were contenders most of the other years. In 1953, he fractured his cheekbone and had sixteen bone chips removed. When he came out of the hospital for the playoff game, he threw only one pass in a losing cause.

In 1954, Y. A. played ten games with

a broken left hand. Later, a chronic groin injury continued to nag him, and in his first season with the Giants a defensive lineman tackled him, crushing the transverse processes in his vertebrae as if they were eggs.

Ironically, many of Tittle's injuries stemmed from one of his most successful plays—the bootleg. Developed out of a fake handoff to a back going into the line, Tittle would keep the ball and run around end.

In 1962, he suffered a brain concussion going into the end zone on a bootleg. The same year his face was badly cut on a roll-out, yet that was the year Tittle threw 33 touchdown passes, breaking the mark shared by Johnny Unitas and Sonny Jurgensen. In the first game of 1963, Tittle's lung was collapsed by a vicious tackle during a bootleg. Similar plays against Green Bay and Dallas also caused back injuries, which eventually hobbled the great passer.

But Tittle always fought back. How well he did was shown in a game he played in 1962, immediately following one in which he had suffered a concussion and hurt his right elbow. He did not participate in practice all that week, as the Giants prepared for their game against the Washington Redskins, who were undefeated and leading the Eastern Division. But when the day of the game arrived, Tittle went up to Sherman and said he was ready.

He started and the day turned into Tittle's greatest as a pro. It also provided a good clue as to the kind of man Y. A. Tittle was in other ways. When the game was over, Tittle had fired seven touchdown passes to triumph over the Redskins, 49–34, and tie a National Football League record. He completed 27 of 39 passes for 505 yards, which remains the second-best mark in NFL history. At one point, he passed for 12 completions in a row.

In the fourth quarter, however, leading 42–20, Tittle really revealed his character. He expected to be rested, but Sherman told Y. A. to stay in there, knowing he was only one touchdown pass away from the record. "You don't get a chance at a record like this very often," his coach told him.

After moving the Giants to the Redskins' 5-yard line, Tittle called for a running play. "C'mon, Yat," urged Alex Webster, the fullback, "go for a pass."

"They'll be expecting a pass," said Tittle, "and besides, I don't want to show 'em up with a record."

Then Frank Gifford, the flanker, spoke up: "If you don't call a pass, Y. A., we're walking off the field."

Tittle gave in, sending Joe Walton, his tight end, toward the right corner of the end zone. He led him perfectly and connected with a pass—and the record.

Although Tittle was an outstanding quarterback with the 49ers, he never achieved the fame and success that he later found with the Giants. The reason was simple: defense.

Tittle had played with a number of fine players at San Francisco, forming one of the all-time great backfields there with Joe Perry, John Henry Johnson, and Hugh McElhenny, whom Tittle called the greatest runner he had ever seen. Nevertheless, the 49ers' defense was not invincible, and the team record proved it.

During his West Coast tenure, another Tittle "special play," called the "Alley Oop," evolved. It came about quite by accident in a practice session one day, when Tittle, trapped by a horde of rushers, flung the ball high into the air, not aiming at anyone. On the San Francisco team was R. C. Owens, an end, who had been an experienced basketball rebounder in college. Though Owens was surrounded by three other players when the ball came down, he leaped up and caught it. "That's our Alley Oop play!" someone yelled.

Tittle found that no matter how high he threw the ball, Owens was almost always able to outjump the defense and catch it. In a game, they would sáve the play for a strategic moment. Suddenly, Tittle would call for the Alley Oop, Owens would plant himself in the end zone, Tittle woud arch the ball toward the crowd Owens had attracted, and Owens would come down with the ball. Many a game was won that way, including the one in 1957 that earned the 49ers a tie for the division championship.

Tittle was traded to the Giants, however, when the 49ers decided to change their offense to the shotgun, where the passer gets the snap from center six or seven yards back and has a choice of running or passing. With a brilliant youngster in their fold—John Brodie—and desperate for help in the line, the 49ers traded Tittle for a rookie guard named Lou Cordileone in what turned out to be one of the more one-sided transactions of all time. Even Cordileone, who had never achieved stardom, remarked: "Me for Tittle? Just me?"

The Giants, with Sam Huff, Dick Modzelewski, Andy Robustelli, and Jim Katcavage anchoring their defense, perfectly complemented Tittle's pinpoint passing attack, and together they piled up three straight Eastern Division championships (1961, 1962, 1963). But their hope for the league title was never realized. Twice they were foiled by the Green Bay Packers under Vince Lombardi, and once by the Chicago Bears.

During those three years, Tittle first backed up Charlie Conerly, then alternated with him before actually becoming No. 1. It was also during this three-year stretch that the passing combination of Tittle and Del Shofner became one of the most potent in the league. The fleet-footed Shofner was on the receiving end of many of

Tittle uses three-quarter delivery to fire ball in '63 title game.

Willie Davis of Packers claws at Tittle after Giants' quarterback has released ball during 1961 championship game won by Green Bay, 37-0.

Tittle's record 36 touchdown passes in 1963.

In the 1963 title game against the Bears, the Giants were favored and seemed to have their best chance at winning the championship. But Lady Luck did not smile on them that day. On a touchdown pass to Gifford in the first quarter, Tittle was hit across the leg by Larry Morris of the Bears. Before long, the leg stiffened, and Tittle began to have trouble dropping back to pass.

Just before the half, Morris again hit Tittle in the leg, this time leaving him virtually helpless. In the second half, Tittle, knowing that only a rookie was backing him up, played on in sheer determination, but he could not engineer a winning formula.

A murderous blitz at the beginning of the next season by a Pittsburgh Steeler defensive end, John Baker, cracked Tittle's ribs and convinced Y. A. that he could no longer be of aid to the Giants, and he retired. Though disappointed and frustrated, old Y. A. Tittle went out as one of the most respected athletes of his time.

"There's no finer person in all of football," remarked Ed Henke, a San Francisco teammate. "The best thing you can take out of this game is to have played with Y. A."

All-America Conference

Year	Team	Games	Att.	Comp.	Pct.	Yards	TDs	Long	Int.	Pct. Int.	Avg. Gain
1948	Balt.	14	289	161	55.7	2522	16		9	3.1	8.73
1949	Balt.	11	289	148	51.2	2209	14		18	6.2	7.64
Totals	2 yrs.	25	578	309	53.5	4731	30		27	4.7	8.19

National Football League

Year	Team	Games	Att.	Comp.	Pct.	Yards	TDs	Long	Int.	Pct. Int.	Avg. Gain
1950	Balt.	12	315	161	51.1	1884	8	62	19	6.0	5.98
1951	S.F.	12	114	63	55.3	808	8	t48	9	7.9	7.09
1952	S.F.	12	208	106	51.0	1407	11	77	12	5.8	6.76
1953	S.F.	9	259	149	57.5	2121	20	71	16	6.2	8.19
1954	S.F.	12	295	170	57.6	2205	9	68	9	3.1	7.47
1955	S.F.	12	287	147	51.2	2185	17	t78	28	9.8	7.61
1956	S.F.	10	218	124	56.9	1641	7	t77	12	5.5	7.53
1957	S.F.	12	279	176	63.1	2157	13	t46	15	5.4	7.73
1958	S.F.	11	208	120	57.7	1467	9	t64	15	7.2	7.05
1959	S.F.	11	199	102	51.3	1331	10	t75	15	7.5	6.69
1960	S.F.	9	127	69	54.3	694	4	45	3	2.4	5.46
1961	N.Y.G.	13	285	163	57.2	2272	17	62	12	4.2	7.97
1962	N.Y.G.	14	375	200	53.3	3224	33	t69	20	5.3	8.60
1963	N.Y.G.	13	367	221	60.2	3145	36	t70	14	3.8	8.57
1964	N.Y.G.	14	281	147	52.3	1798	10	54	22	7.8	6.40
Totals	15 yrs.	176	3817	2118	55.5	28,339	212	t78	221	5.8	7.42

Fights off Jim Riley, Dolphins' defensive end, as Bill Stanfill (84), the other end, bears down on Colts' star during 1972 AFC title game.

Johnny Unitas

Johnny Unitas
by Dave Anderson

In the dim light of Mamma Leone's restaurant in New York City, the awards luncheon was about to begin. Johnny Unitas was to be honored as *the* pro football player of the 25-year period from 1946 to 1971, and as he stood in his slouch-shouldered style, his hair longer now than it used to be, his icy blue eyes peering out of his bony face, he was approached by a middle-aged man.

"Could I have your autograph?" the man asked.

"Certainly," replied the Baltimore Colts' quarterback, taking the souvenir menu and pen.

"It's for my garageman," the stranger said.

"For *who,* sir?" Unitas asked, not quite understanding him in the babble of voices around them.

UPI
Unitas gets rid of ball before Ben Davidson of Raiders (83) and Tony Cline (84) smother him in 1971 AFC championship game.

Unitas throws over arms of Packers' trio—Clarence Williams (83), Mike McCoy (76), Kevin Hardy—and to a Baltimore pass-catcher.

"My garageman," the man repeated. "He thinks you're the greatest football player of all time."

Unitas smiled and joked, "I'm big with the garagemen."

But the essence of Johnny Unitas might best be symbolized by the admiration of that garageman. In its basics, football—particularly pro football—is a game that a garageman probably identifies with better than most workers in this society. It's a game of hard toil, of dirt under the fingernails, of blood and broken bones, of casual recognition for virtual perfection, of damning blame for mistakes.

Being "big with the garagemen" might be considered more of a tribute to Johnny Unitas than all of his trophies and awards.

His stature is secure. In the days prior to the 1971 American Football Conference championship game, Don Shula, coach of the Miami Dolphins and once a coach of the Colts, was asked to compare Unitas with his current quarterback, Bob Griese. Unitas was then thirty-eight years old, his right heel scarred from Achilles-tendon surgery less than a year earlier, his passing arm weary after sixteen seasons.

"Griese is one of the fine young quarterbacks," Shula said, "but Unitas is *the* quarterback."

The distance of his passing gains can be measured in miles. That's miles, not yards. More than twenty-one miles through the 1971 season, or 38,657 yards on 2,708 completions in 4,953 attempts for 283 touchdowns. He once threw at least one touchdown pass in forty-seven consecutive games. He has thrown for more than three hundred yards in twenty-five games.

"It's like being in the huddle with God," says John Mackey, the NFL's all-time tight end.

His stature among teammates is unchallenged. Although he is now their teammate, he was *the* quarterback when many of the current Colts were in college, when some were in high school, when the youngest Colts were in grammar school. Eddie Hinton, a wide receiver who was the Colts' first-round draft choice in 1969, was only eleven years old when Unitas directed the Colts to their famous sudden-death overtime victory over the New York Giants for the 1958 NFL title. When Hinton joined the Colts as a rookie, he was catching the ball for Unitas in the sideline warm-up when the quarterback noticed him peeking out from behind his facemask.

"What's the matter, Eddie?"

"I can't believe it's you."

"You're just getting old."

No matter how old anybody gets, the 1958 sudden-death victory will be cherished as Johnny Unitas's finest hour. The Colts were losing, 17–14, to the Giants in the dusk at Yankee Stadium, with the scoreboard clock blinking 1:56—one minute, fifty-six seconds to play. And the Colts were 86 yards from the Giant goal line. As the Colts' punt-return unit trotted off the field, the offense trotted on. Unitas buckled his chin strap and lowered his white helmet with the blue horseshoes on it into the huddle.

"Now we're going to find out what we're made of," he said in his icy, sharp voice. "Unless the clock is stopped, we won't have time for any more huddles. Stay alert. I'll call the plays at the line."

On the first play, Unitas found Lenny Moore, his slinky running back, with a pass for an 11-yard gain. First down at the 25. After the Colts had lined up quickly without a huddle, Unitas completed another pass to wide receiver Raymond Berry for a 25-yard gain. First down at midfield. Again without a huddle, Unitas passed to Berry for a 15-yard gain. First down at the Giants' 35. As the seconds continued to flash on the scoreboard clock, Unitas found Berry again for a 22-yard gain to the Giants' 13. From the sideline, Steve Myhra, the Colts' place-kicker, ran out to attempt the tying field goal.

At the 20-yard line, Myhra swung his foot and the ball spun between the uprights, tying the score at 17–17. The scoreboard clock showed seven seconds remaining.

Until this game, the NFL never had a tie in one of its championships. But in anticipation of the possibility, the league had formulated a sudden-death overtime. If there was a tie after the regulation sixty minutes, the game would continue with fifteen-minute quarters, ending when one team scored in any manner—touchdown, field goal, or safety.

The Colts lost the coin-toss and kicked off, but their defensive unit quickly forced the Giants to punt.

Again the Colts had the ball deep in their own territory, at the 20-yard line. But this time Unitas had time to call plays in the huddle. Slowly, surely, he directed the Colts across midfield and into Giant territory. Soon the Colts had a second down at the Giants' 8, but there Unitas chose a daring play—a pass to tight end Jim Mutscheller near the sideline. Had a Giant defender intercepted, he might have run the length of the field for the winning touchdown. But the pass was completed to Mutscheller at the 1. On third down, Unitas chose a running play, a handoff to running back Alan ("The Horse") Ameche, who smashed into the end zone. Since the Colts had scored, the extra point was unnecessary. Final score: 23–17.

Even now, thousands of games later, it is rated by many pro-football aficionados as "the greatest game ever played."

As its star, Johnny Unitas was surrounded by newsmen at his locker in the Yankee Stadium catacombs. His white jersey with the big blue "19" was streaked with dirt and grass stains. So were his gray pants. But he was smiling.

"That pass to Mutscheller," one of the newsmen asked. "Weren't you risking an interception there?"

"When you know what you're doing," Unitas said with a serious smile, "you don't get intercepted."

Put it on his Hall of Fame plaque. In those few words, Johnny Unitas described what makes him tick. Not that he has never been intercepted. During the 1971 season, he threw 240 interceptions. But the important thing is that he never permitted an interception to undermine his confidence as a quarterback. During a 1970 game with the Chicago Bears he had five passes intercepted, but he sparked a 21–20 victory. When he was asked about the interceptions, he shrugged.

"They happen," he said.

He has the same detached attitude toward touchdown passes. Against the Houston Oilers, in the 1970 season, the Colts were trailing, 20–17, in the final minute. With the ball at the Oilers' 31, he moved quickly in his bowlegged manner, his high-top black shoes shuffling on the bright green Astro-Turf surface of the Astrodome, and whipped a long pass to Roy Jefferson, a wide receiver streaking along the right sideline.

After he threw the ball, Unitas turned toward the Colts' bench. He never saw Jefferson catch the pass for a touchdown with 46 seconds remaining. The Colts won, 24–20.

In the locker room later, Don Klosterman, the Colts' general manager, asked Unitas why he had turned away when he threw the pass, why he hadn't bothered to watch Jefferson catch the ball, why he had been so certain that Jefferson would catch it.

"He's paid to catch it," the quarterback replied.

That's the philosophy of a pure profes-

Unitas has just passed as his center, Bill Curry, is on lookout for any intruders.

sional. But the scary thing about the career of Johnny Unitas as *the* quarterback is that it almost never happened. Until he clicked with the Colts in the 1956 season, he had always been the quarterback nobody wanted.

Born on May 7, 1933, in Pittsburgh, Pennsylvania, he was one of four children whose mother kept their father's coal-trucking business going for a few months after his death. She also worked at night, scrubbing floors in downtown Pittsburgh office buildings. She later worked in a bakery and sold insurance while studying bookkeeping at night.

"In her civil service exam," her famous son says proudly, "she got the highest mark in her class. My mother never really liked

football, but she taught me more about it, by her example of what it takes to get ahead, than any of my coaches. And I've had some good coaches."

But his mother couldn't afford to pay for his college tuition. He needed an athletic scholarship. He was the all-Catholic quarterback in the Pittsburgh area at St. Justin's High School, but he was a skinny 145 pounds. Notre Dame turned him down as too small. So did Indiana, Maryland, and Lehigh. But searching desperately for a scholarship, he attended a tryout at the University of Louisville.

"You can throw the ball," the coach, Frank Camp, told him. "I think you'll put on some weight. You got yourself a free ride."

87

Unitas on a nine-yard run up the middle
is nailed by Packers' Henry Jordan.

He had his scholarship: tuition, board, room, books, fees, and $25 a month for laundry and incidentals. He also had his opportunity. Louisville was not a member of the National Collegiate Athletic Association at the time, so freshmen were eligible for varsity competition. Midway through his freshman season in 1951, he took over as the first-string quarterback in a game against St. Bonaventure's and threw for three touchdowns as his passes gained more than 300 yards. By the end of his senior year, his four-year record was 245 completions in 502 passes for 2,912 yards and 27 touchdowns. He had filled out physically, too, into a six-foot-one-inch, 195-pounder with wiry strength.

On the day of the NFL draft, his hometown Pittsburgh Steelers selected him in the eighth round. But after a few weeks at their training camp at Olean, New York, he was released. Three other experienced quarterbacks—Jim Finks, Ted Marchibroda and Vic Eaton—were kept by the Steeler coach, Walt Kiesling.

"What was the matter with Unitas?" Kiesling was asked by one of the Steeler executives.

"Too dumb," the coach replied. "The kid was just too dumb to be a pro quarterback."

Unitas hitchhiked home, disappointed but typically undaunted. He got in touch with the Cleveland Browns, who were having quarterback problems because Otto Graham had retired. But what Unitas didn't know was that Paul Brown, then the Browns' coach, was persuading Graham to postpone his retirement until the next year.

89

"No need for you this season," Brown answered in a telegram. "Suggest you come to camp next summer for tryout. Please contact me in the spring."

Encouraged by the future opportunity, Unitas joined the Bloomfield Rams, a Pittsburgh semi-pro team, at $6 a game to supplement his income working on a pile driver. Then, one day in February, 1956, his phone rang. In retrospect, the telephone call has emerged as one of the most significant in NFL history.

"This is Don Kellett, general manager of the Baltimore Colts," the voice said. "We'd like to take a look at you."

The Colts were short on quarterbacks. They had an experienced starter in George Shaw, but their backup quarterback, Gary Kerkorian, had retired from pro football to enter law school.

"We're having a tryout camp here in Baltimore in May," Kellett continued. "We'd like you to come down to it and work out."

At the tryout camp, Unitas impressed Colt coach Weeb Ewbank, and when the full squad reported to training camp, Ewbank chose Unitas as his backup quarterback.

In an early season game against the Bears in Chicago, Shaw suffered a knee injury. The Colts were leading, 21–20, when Unitas took over. He could not have done worse. He fumbled three handoffs and the Bears turned each one into a touchdown. He overthrew a receiver and the Bears returned the interception for another touchdown. The Bears won, 58–27.

"Forget about it," Ewbank advised. "You're the quarterback next week. You can play in this league."

In his next game, Unitas threw two touchdown passes against the Green Bay Packers. Then the Colts routed the Los Angeles Rams, 56–21. He was secure now at quarterback. The following season the Colts finished third in the NFL's Western Division, then in 1958 and 1959 they won NFL championships. Suddenly he was the quarterback *everybody* wanted. He has been voted the NFL's most valuable player three times—in 1957, 1964, and 1967. He was the all-NFL quarterback six times. He has been a member of the Pro Bowl all-star squad ten times.

Not that he's infallible. Twice he failed to get the Colts on the scoreboard in championship games—the 21–6 loss to the Dolphins for the 1971 AFC title and the 27–0 loss to the Browns for the 1964 NFL title.

But nobody's perfect. Perhaps his most dramatic scenario developed in the 1971 season. On an April day that year, he was playing paddle tennis with Tom Matte, the Colt running back, when the Achilles tendon in his right heel snapped. Driven to a nearby hospital by Matte, he phoned Don Klosterman at the Colt offices.

"They're going to operate right away, tonight," Unitas said. "I don't know what to tell you now."

Momentarily, he was concerned about his future as a competitor, but only because he didn't know the extent of the injury. Later that night, assured that he could return if he complied with the necessary therapy, he assured Klosterman, too.

"I'll be there for the opener, I'll be all right," Unitas said. "But for now, get me a beer."

Klosterman grinned. But like most people, he thought that Unitas was too optimistic. Very few athletes recover in five months from Achilles-tendon surgery. It's one of the most damaging injuries in sports because the entire balance of the foot is affected and the tendon itself is slow to heal. For a quarterback who needs quick feet to set up and strong feet to throw off, it's even more damaging. But the last thing that Johnny Unitas wanted was sympathy.

In famous 1958 sudden-death NFL title game, Unitas swings to his right as Colt blockers
try to cope with Jim Katcavage and Dick Modzelewski of Giants.

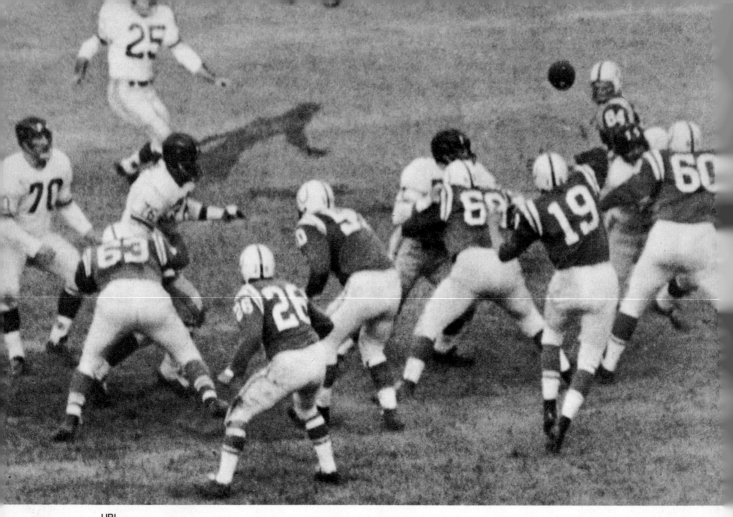

Unitas pitches to Jim Mutscheller (above, next to ball) and Colts' tight end gathers in ball (below) in a quick over-the-middle maneuver for a first down on Giants' 25 in second quarter of 1959 title game at Baltimore.

As Colts' halfback breaks out of backfield, Unitas lofts ball over Packers' leaping Willie Davis (87) while Ron Kostelnik (77) rushes in to pressure Baltimore quarterback.

Unitas, on a rare running play, scores in 1959 championship game as Giants' Jim Katcavage and Dick Modzelewski (77) pursue Baltimore hero in vain.

"You can win the Comeback of the Year award," somebody suggested.

"Comeback, hell," he said with his marvelous sneer, "I ain't been away!"

Still limping, he reported to training camp on time. And when the Colts opened their season, he was on the forty-player active list. By mid-season, with the Colts struggling, he replaced Earl Morrall at quarterback in a game with the Jets at New York, and directed them to two touchdowns for a 14–13 victory. Two weeks after that, he directed a 14–3 triumph over the Dolphins that assured the Colts of an AFC playoff berth. Early in that game, he flipped a short pass to Matte, his buddy who was all alone near the sideline. Matte dropped it. As the experienced running back returned to the huddle, he noticed Unitas glaring at him from inside his face mask.

"Catch the ball, Matte," the quarterback snapped.

Significantly, none of Unitas' next ten passes was dropped as the Colts took command. Instead of trying to force his passes through the deep areas of the Dolphins' zone defense, he tossed short, quick passes, many to his running backs, in two touchdown drives that resembled excerpts from a coach's manual.

"You take what they give you," Unitas said. "They always give you something and you try to take it."

But not every quarterback can recognize what the opposing defense is giving him. And not every quarterback is able to take it. No quarterback can do it in every game, not even Johnny Unitas. But through the seasons with different coaches and different teammates, he has done it more often than any other quarterback.

"Johnny Unitas is the greatest quarterback to ever play the game," Sid Luckman once said. "He's better than me, better than Sammy Baugh, better than anyone."

Year	Team	Games	Att.	Comp.	Pct.	Yards	TDs	Long	Int.	Pct. Int.	Avg. Gain
1956	Balt.	12	198	110	55.6	1498	9	54	10	5.1	7.57
1957	Balt.	12	301	172	57.1	2550	24	t82	17	5.6	8.47
1958	Balt.	10	263	136	51.7	2007	19	77	7	2.7	7.63
1959	Balt.	12	367	193	52.6	2899	32	71	14	3.8	7.90
1960	Balt.	12	378	190	50.3	3099	25	t80	24	6.3	8.20
1961	Balt.	14	420	229	54.5	2990	16	t72	24	5.7	7.12
1962	Balt.	14	389	222	57.1	2967	23	t80	23	5.9	7.63
1963	Balt.	14	410	237	57.8	3481	20	t64	12	2.9	8.49
1964	Balt.	14	305	158	51.8	2824	19	t74	6	2.0	9.26
1965	Balt.	11	282	164	58.2	2530	23	61	12	4.3	8.97
1966	Balt.	14	348	195	56.0	2748	22	t89	24	6.9	7.90
1967	Balt.	14	436	255	58.5	3428	20	t88	16	3.7	7.86
1968	Balt.	5	32	11	34.4	139	2	37	4	12.5	4.34
1969	Balt.	13	327	178	54.4	2342	12	t52	20	6.1	7.16
1970	Balt.	14	321	166	51.7	2213	14	t55	18	5.6	6.89
1971	Balt.	13	176	92	52.3	942	3	35	9	5.1	5.35
Totals 16 yrs.		**198**	**4953**	**2708**	**54.7**	**38,657**	**283**	**t89**	**240**	**4.8**	**7.80**

Spirals ball to Green Bay teammate in 1967 title game against Cowboys.

Bart Starr

Bart Starr

by George DeGregorio

When the 50,861 dedicated pro-football "Eskimos" began to drift into the igloo that was Lambeau Field that day in Green Bay, Wisconsin, the temperature was 14 degrees below zero. They had paid $12 a ticket for the hoped-for pleasure of watching the Packers beat the Dallas Cowboys for a third straight National Football League championship.

The Packers—proud warriors goaded on by their General Patton-like coach, Vince Lombardi—relied above all on their disciplined and unyielding quarterback, Bryan Bartlett Starr, the part-Cherokee Indian son of an Air Force master sergeant. Their intention was to become the first team in the forty-seven year history of the NFL to win the league title three years in succession. Starr's goal: to become the only NFL quarterback to lead his team to five league championships.

Starr confers with Coach Vince Lombardi during Super Bowl I.

98

Because a victory would shower Starr and the Packers with unprecedented accolades, this was as important a game as the Packers would ever play. Not even the first two Super Bowl games would better typify the qualities that had made Starr a flawless quarterback, a genius at play execution.

While the fans shivered in the cold, Bart Starr, once derisively called an "automaton" by Bobby Layne, began reading the Cowboy defenses on the frozen turf. And in the first eighteen minutes he clicked with two touchdown passes and a 14–0 lead for his team.

The year before, Starr had led the Packers over the Cowboys, 34–27, for a second straight league crown before 75,-500 fans in Dallas. In a rare departure from his usual self-effacing, modest manner, Starr was seen afterward in the club's dressing room, embracing his rather quiet teammates and exclaiming, "How sweet it is, how sweet it is!"

The Cowboys this time were determined to put a rope on this runaway steer and return him to his proper humility.

The Dallas front four began zeroing in on Starr, sacking him eight times for a loss of 76 yards. Willie Townes dropped Starr for a 19-yard loss, forcing a fumble that was recovered by George Andrie, who ran it in for a touchdown from the 7. Then, moments before the half ended, Danny Villanueva kicked a 21-yard field goal and the Cowboys were back in contention, 14–10, trailing by only four points.

Outplaying the Packers for forty of the sixty minutes, the Cowboys got a big play early in the fourth quarter. Dan Reeves, a halfback, passed to Lance Rentzel, a flanker who had roamed unseen into the clear, for 50 yards and a touchdown, completely fooling the Packers.

But with five minutes left to play, Starr began throwing short passes to his backs, Donny Anderson and Chuck Mercein. The Cowboy linebackers covering them complained that the frozen ground afforded them no traction so that the advantage on the field "had gone to the offense." Starr had read things right.

The big play in Starr's fusillade was a 19-yard aerial to Mercein to the Cowboy 11. On the next play Mercein stormed to the 3, but in two plays Anderson succeeded only in reaching the 1. With a third-and-one situation, and only thirteen seconds left on the clock, Starr gathered the Packers into a huddle.

He took extra time to explain what he wanted. He said he wanted the same blocking as always and that he wouldn't hand off to either the halfback or the fullback.

"We darn well better make it," he said.

The Packers got the message. Starr took the ball and blasted over right guard, behind Jerry Kramer's key block, for the winning score. The Packers had taken it all, 21–17.

The victory and the way it was achieved, more than any other, was the culmination of Starr's quarterbacking genius.

This time Starr, the NFL's most valuable player the previous year, had drawn upon his ten years of experience—all he had learned in a career marked by big frustrations as well as memorable victories. Even the elements often seemed to conspire against him, making the sixty minutes of a football game as complicated as life.

His hands numb, his ribs aching, Starr always maintained a grace under pressure that would have made grist for Hemingway's mill. Another quarterback, tackled eight times for losses, might have given up in despair. Another quarterback, seeing the Packer lead go up in smoke on a fake-out play, might have lost control. Another quarterback, more desperate and inclined to gamble, might have tried for the long bomb.

Starr's ability that day to capitalize on the condition of the turf and get the ball moving in the last five minutes was a classic example of his instant reasoning on the field even in the most difficult of circumstances.

He moved the Packers 68 yards on short passes and short running plays. Nothing spectacular, but every yard was fought for and won as if the game depended on it—and it did. Starr had stamped his brand indelibly on this particular game, and he alone determined how it would be won.

His masterful direction of the Packers in their first Super Bowl victory over the Kansas City Chiefs the previous January had gone a long way to mark him as a "super-Starr." But he had really been that all the time without due and proper recognition. He proved it again in the second Super Bowl triumph over the Oakland Raiders.

The journey to greatness for Bart Starr, who was born in Montgomery, Alabama, on January 9, 1934, was beset by mental anguish. While he always showed flashes of brilliance, his career, even in college, took twists and turns that resembled a ride on a roller coaster.

As a freshman quarterback at Alabama he gained national attention when he helped the Crimson Tide rout Syracuse in the 1953 Orange Bowl, 61–6. The next season he led 'Bama to the Cotton Bowl. Then, in his junior year, a back injury put him out of action.

Ready to make a big comeback as a senior, Starr found himself warming the bench instead. A new coach was trying out a new experiment—a 'Bama team composed chiefly of sophomores and juniors —and Starr was out.

The demotion was a bitter pill for Starr, and he has said that he survived the humiliation only because he got married in his junior year. "My wife was a wonderful

UPI
Tries to ward off Rams' Roger Brown (above).

UPI
John Zook of Falcons clutches Starr but he grabs face mask (he was penalized).

Starr set to pass as John Brockington (42) and Wimpy Winther (52) guard him.

help. For a young person, she has a lot of maturity."

His credentials as a passer at Alabama —155 completions in 285 attempts for 1,093 yards—were valid enough, but he was only a seventeenth-round draft choice (199th of all eligible players) of the Packers in 1956.

But the loss of confidence he experienced at Alabama was kid stuff compared to the ordeal of frustration he was to undergo at Green Bay. Except for his Packer roommate, Tobin Rote, who would be traded away after the season, and Babe Parilli, one of Starr's boyhood idols, the Packers were a nondescript bunch.

When Starr arrived in summer camp, the team had won six and lost six the previous season. Starr managed to win a second-string job behind Rote, although he had to

sweat out the cut (there were five quarterbacks in camp) until the last day.

He was only a part-time quarterback for the next two losing campaigns. But he gained some notice in a game against the Colts in the dreary 1958 season, completing 26 of 46 passes for 320 yards, although the Packers lost by a touchdown and finished with a horrendous 1–10–1 record.

The losing streak did not help Starr, already short on confidence, and the Packer management, disenchanted with a team that registered the worst record in the club's history, brought in Vince Lombardi as coach. Lombardi had been a high school coach, an assistant for the New York Giants, an aide to Red Blaik at Army, and one of the "Seven Blocks of Granite" at Fordham in the 1930's.

What Lombardi's dossier could not show

102

was his fierce determination to succeed. Like Starr, Lombardi considered himself deprived of a chance to show his skills. Now he had the opportunity to transform a loser into a winner, but the quarterback was his big problem.

Unknown to Starr, the arrival of Lombardi would further put off the day when he would become a regular performer. For the sensitive nonsmoking, nondrinking kid from Alabama, it would still be a waiting game filled with self-doubt and uncertainty.

The movies taken of the 1958 Packers did not impress Lombardi, and one of his first decisions was to trade for Lamar Mc-Han, a journeyman signal-caller with the St. Louis Cardinals. The acquisition of Mc-Han came as a blow to Starr, who supposed that with a new coach and changes in personnel he might move up to a position of leadership. Starr's confidence was shattered again.

Trying to rationalize the move, Starr told a friend, "I don't blame Coach Lombardi for trading for Lamar. The Packers do need a quarterback. I haven't been doing the job. And now it looks like maybe I never will."

Yet he was to become the passer who set the NFL record for throwing 294 consecutive passes without an interception.

"You have a quick way of understanding defenses and offenses," Lisle Blackbourn, his first Green Bay coach, told him. "You learn fast. But I think you'd make a better teacher of quarterbacks. You are going to have a tough time making it as a pro."

Starr's answer was, "No, thanks, I'm going to try to make it as a pro quarterback." The decision must have kept him awake many a night.

Starr was to have salt rubbed into his wounds one more time before he could win the favor of Lombardi, who on first inspection had dismissed Starr as being too sensitive to be the authoritarian quarterback he envisioned for the Packers.

It occurred midway in the 1959 season. McHan suffered a shoulder separation before the Packer game with the Giants in Yankee Stadium. The Packers had opened with three straight victories, then dropped the next two. The Giant game was important to Lombardi. As a native New Yorker and a former Giants' offensive coach, he was eager to give his old friends a run for the money.

When it became evident that McHan couldn't throw, Lombardi's choice to replace him was Joe Francis, a converted tailback with only a smattering of experience and distinguishable only in that he had two first names. The Giants' defense tore Francis to pieces and the Packers lost, 20–3.

Starr said later, "I thought, boy, this was going to be my big chance. So I worked real hard all week and thought I had everything down cold. I had a good game plan. So what does he [Lombardi] do when it's evident early in the game Mac can't throw? He sticks Joe Francis in there.

"I was so sick and disgusted, I couldn't see straight. I was so mad after the game I went out with Ron Kramer, another benchwarmer, and we cried on each other's shoulder. Only time in my life I really felt sorry for myself."

In light of the debacle in New York, Lombardi must have had a quick change of heart. The next week McHan injured a leg and Starr got the starting assignment against the Chicago Bears. He played regularly the rest of the season, and in the last four games he had 52 completions in 79 attempts for 699 yards. The Packers won all four and posted their first winning season (7–5) in twelve years.

At last the "marriage" of Bart Starr and Vince Lombardi began to work. The

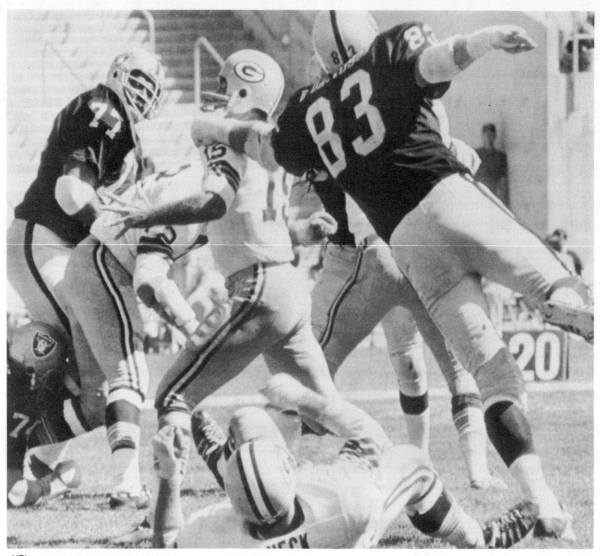

Starr manages to fling pass as Raiders' Ben Davidson hooks him by the left shoulder.

courtship had been strained, but they were two of a kind—more than anything else, they both wanted to succeed. The honeymoon was long and beautiful.

The desire to succeed, to fulfill himself, undoubtedly was what made Bart Starr a perfectionist. During the next eight seasons he was at the helm as the Packers won the Western Conference title six times, the NFL crown five times, and the Super Bowl twice.

The victory over the Cowboys in 1967 was especially sweet for Starr because it was achieved with a team that for the most part was old, injured, and ailing. The

Packers of 1966, who had a 12–2 record, were considered a better team (eight of them made all-pro).

In the 1967 season, and often throughout his career, Starr played in constant pain with a multitude of injuries (Lombardi had no sympathy for "little hurts"), wearing a special corset to protect aching ribs; he also had knee problems and a broken hand.

A broken hand also sidelined him for five games in 1963. He missed 28 quarters with rib injuries in 1968 and 27 quarters in 1969 with a shoulder separation suffered against the Lions with four games

104

to go in the season. In 1970 he was out 16 quarters, and in 1971 numerous old maladies cropped up to impair his effectiveness.

Nevertheless, he compiled one of the greatest career passing records in all of pro football, completing a higher percentage of passes than any NFL player, including Unitas, Graham, Tittle, Baugh, and Luckman.

Through 1970 he had completed 1,784 passes in 3,104 attempts for 23,432 yards and 152 touchdowns—a percentage figure of 57.5. He was the leading passer in the NFL in 1962, 1964, and 1966; most valuable player in 1966; and most valuable player in each of the first two Super Bowl games. His 294 consecutive pass attempts without a theft attest to his magnificent control under pressure.

Two days before the Packers' final game of the 1971 season, a brief news dispatch appeared on one of the wire services.

It read:

MIAMI, December 17 (UPI)—Green Bay Packer coach Dan Devine said today he would start veteran quarterback Bart Starr in Sunday's game against the Miami Dolphins. He announced his choice after a 70-minute workout on artificial turf at the Orange Bowl.

That item must have been read with disenchantment by those who remembered the day Bart Starr, the "American Gothic" of pro football, put one over for the Packers in the dank cold of Lambeau Field.

Now at thirty-seven, after sixteen seasons as a Packer, Bart Starr had come full-circle. Now Bart Starr, with a wife and two young sons and with very little to prove on the football field any more, found himself in the tenuous position of trying to win his spurs again. The 1971 Packers finished with a 4–8–2 mark, their worst since 1958.

But this time, with Vince Lombardi gone, and all the Packers virtually retired, the man to decide whether Starr would start one more time was a former Missouri college coach in his rookie season with the pros.

Maybe Bart Starr had heard his last hurrah, but found it too hard to accept.

Year	Team	Games	Att.	Comp.	Pct.	Yards	TDs	Long	Int.	Pct. Int.	Avg. Gain
1956	G.B.	9	44	24	54.5	325	2	t39	3	6.8	7.39
1957	G.B.	12	215	117	54.4	1489	8	t77	10	4.7	6.93
1958	G.B.	12	157	78	49.7	845	3	t55	12	7.6	5.38
1959	G.B.	12	134	70	52.2	972	6	t44	7	5.2	7.25
1960	G.B.	12	172	98	57.0	1358	4	t91	8	4.7	7.90
1961	G.B.	14	295	172	58.3	2418	16	t78	16	5.4	8.20
1962	G.B.	14	285	178	62.5	2438	12	t83	9	3.2	8.55
1963	G.B.	13	244	132	54.1	1855	15	t53	10	4.1	7.60
1964	G.B.	14	272	163	59.9	2144	15	73	4	1.5	7.88
1965	G.B.	14	251	140	55.8	2055	16	t77	9	3.6	8.19
1966	G.B.	14	251	156	62.2	2257	14	t83	3	1.2	8.99
1967	G.B.	14	210	115	54.8	1823	9	84	17	8.1	8.68
1968	G.B.	12	171	109	63.7	1617	15	t63	8	4.7	9.46
1969	G.B.	12	148	92	62.2	1161	9	51	6	4.1	7.84
1970	G.B.	14	255	140	54.9	1645	8	t65	13	5.1	6.45
1971	G.B.	4	45	24	53.3	286	0	31	3	6.7	6.36
Totals 16 yrs.		196	3149	1808	57.4	24,688	152	t91	138	4.4	7.84

Tucks the ball in and seeks an avenue of escape as Cowboys' George
Andrie (66), Pat Toomay (67), and Jethro Pugh (75) converge on him.

Sonny Jurgensen

Sonny Jurgensen
by Deane McGowen

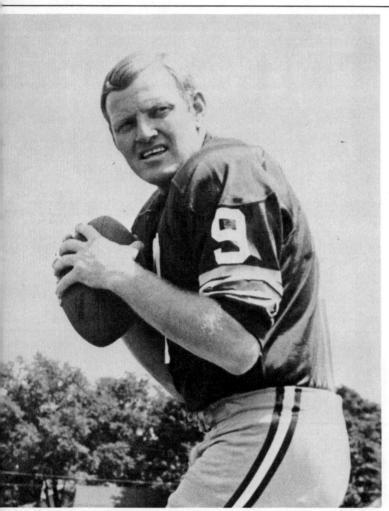

Nat Fine photo

The National Football League has worked out a statistical formula to determine season and all-time rankings among quarterbacks. There are four categories in which the passers are rated: highest completion percentage, most touchdown passes, lowest percentage of interceptions, and highest average gain per attempt.

Amazingly, right at the top of the career list (for those who have thrown more than 1,500 passes) is Christian Adolph ("Sonny") Jurgensen of the Washington Redskins. The supreme irony is that, despite his talents, he has yet to compete in a playoff or championship game! His story somewhat parallels that of Walter Johnson, another star thrower for a Washington club, the baseball Senators. One of the greatest right-handed pitchers in history, Johnson played well for many years without toeing

Wide World
Jurgensen passes and A.D. Whitfield knifes through air to stop Eagles' Mel Tom (58), who attempts to hurtle Redskins' back.

108

the mound in a World Series game until late in his career.

Jurgensen's bad luck almost came to an end in 1969 when the fabled Vince Lombardi took over as the Redskins' coach. Under Lombardi's iron discipline and dedicated coaching, the fortunes of the Redskins immediately turned around. They won seven games, lost five, and tied two to make it the first season in fourteen years that they finished over the .500 mark.

Lombardi, depending mainly on Jurgensen's arm, molded the Redskins into winners. Jurgensen did so well on the field that he captured his second NFL passing title in three years. He threw the ball with great accuracy, completing 274 of 442 pass attempts and gaining 3,102 yards. His completion percentage of 62 was the best in the league.

Jurgensen remembers the initial meeting with Lombardi. Lombardi called him into his office and told Jurgensen to be himself. You know—be Vince Lombardi.

As Jurgensen saw the facts, he (Jurgensen) was the activist, the individual, and Lombardi was the Organization. While Lombardi was creating one of pro football's greatest dynasties, the Green Bay Packers, Jurgensen had been breaking individual NFL passing records, first at Philadelphia, then at Washington. Lombardi was a prophet of God, country and percentages. Jurgensen was football's elder swinger and its most accomplished percentage passer. Still, Jurgensen's teams had never won. After that first fine year, Jurgensen said: "Lombardi has given me a new lease on life. I'm no kid, but I'm trying like one." But by the next season, Lombardi had died.

Enter George Allen, another winning coach. In five seasons Allen had coached the Los Angeles Rams to two division titles. Now, in 1971, the Redskins responded to Allen's talent and his relentless enthusiasm by posting a 9–4–1 regular-season record before losing to the San Francisco 49ers in the 1971 playoffs.

But none of this was accomplished with Jurgensen. In the next-to-last pre-season game against the Miami Dolphins, Jurgensen suffered a fractured left shoulder and sat out almost the entire season. It was typical of Jurgensen's career. Every time he stood on the threshold of success, the veteran quarterback experienced a substantial loss.

Christian Adolph Jurgensen, III was born on August 23, 1934, in Wilmington, North Carolina. He was an all-around athlete at New Hanover High School, starring in football, basketball, and baseball.

During his junior year he played middle linebacker on defense and halfback on offense. In his senior year he switched to quarterback and began a career as one of pro football's most gifted passers.

"Our coach, Leon Brogden, had a drill in which I had to get on one knee and throw the ball," Sonny recalled. "It may not seem like much, but I think it developed the strength in my arm and taught me how to really snap the ball the way I do."

Offered many scholarships, Jurgensen settled on Duke University. He emerged four years later with a degree in education and a wealth of experience, not in passing, but in handing off to running backs in Coach Bill Murray's offense. Although Jurgensen helped the Blue Devils to twenty victories, three ties and eight losses, plus a 34–7 triumph over Nebraska in the Orange Bowl, he was not permitted to pass often.

During his sophomore season Jurgensen completed 12 of 28 passes for 212 yards. As a junior, his figures were 37 of 39 for 536. In his final year he hit with 29 for 371 yards. He had only six touchdown passes to show for three varsity seasons, hardly enough to attract a pro scout. But Ace Parker, the former Brooklyn Dodger

Jurgensen passes despite Cowboys' Bob Lilly's efforts.

Jurgensen searches for open man as Cowboys' Andrie and Lilly close in on him.

star who was a member of the Duke coaching staff, recommended Jurgensen to the Philadelphia Eagles. The Eagles drafted Jurgensen on the fourth round in 1957. He was instrumental in three of the Eagles' four victories that season and the club regarded him as a talented, strong-armed prospect.

Then came Norm Van Brocklin. "The Dutchman" arrived from the Rams in 1958, along with Coach Buck Shaw. Van Brocklin played, and Jurgensen sat on the bench or stood at the sidelines with earphones connected to spotters on the stadium roof.

With the caustic, tough-minded Van Brocklin leading them (or goading them), the Eagles began to improve. They tied for second place in the Eastern Division in 1959, then captured the championship against Green Bay in 1960.

"The Dutchman" retired after the 1960 season, and Jurgensen took over as quarterback under a new coach, Nick Skorich. The years of waiting were finally over, and Jurgensen got his chance to establish himself. Eventually, he surpassed many of Van Brocklin's records.

In 1961, his first full season, Jurgensen was spectacular. He completed more than 56 percent of his passes for an average of almost nine yards per attempt. He led the league in completions (235), yards gained (3,723), and touchdown passes (32). By throwing so often, he also led the league in passes intercepted (24).

He almost took the Eagles to a second title. Their 10–4 record in 1962 fell just a half-game short of New York's 10–3–1 mark in the Eastern Division.

That was as close as the roly-poly quarterback ever came to a championship. He was a young man playing with an old team

Nat Fine photo
Jurgensen had happy but, unfortunately, brief teaming up with Coach Vince Lombardi.

in its decline. The Eagles skidded into the cellar the next season at 3–10–1. They remained there in 1963 at 2–10–2.

Jurgensen was blamed for many of the Eagles' problems. Because he had the reputation of partying too much and because he appeared to be overweight, the fans thought he was out of shape. When the Eagles lost, the fans blamed him and showed it by booing him.

"Well, here it is again, fellows," he once said as the fans yelled at him. "You've got 60,000 critics and no private life in this game. I don't let it eat my insides out." His teammate, Timmy Brown, indicated otherwise: "He never let on, but it hurt."

When the Eagles brought in Joe Kuharich as coach, Kuharich traded Jurgensen to Washington for Norm Snead. Then it was the Redskins' turn to struggle with the fun-loving Jurgensen. The team's winning record was mediocre, but Jurgensen compiled some of the most outstanding records in history. His deft touch enabled him to throw the ball long or short, hard or soft, with amazing accuracy against first-rate opposition.

In that first season at Washington, Jurgensen completed 207 passes for 2,934 yards and 24 touchdowns. A year later his figures were 190 passes for 2,367 yards and 15 scores. And in 1966 he broke league records by completing 254 of 436 (more than 58 percent) for 3,200 yards and 28 touchdowns. In 1967 he astounded the league, setting records with 288 completions in 508 attempts (better than 56 percent) for 3,747 yards and a fourth mark with 31 touchdown passes. And his total of interceptions dropped to 16.

In the summer of 1968 Jurgensen underwent an operation for the removal of calcium deposits in his right elbow, so he was unable to play until the final pre-season game. Then, in the fifth game of the season, Jurgensen suffered fractured ribs. Finally, he was stricken with the flu. In all, he missed three full games and major parts of others. Still, he managed to complete 167 passes in 292 attempts for 1,980 yards and 17 touchdowns; and he had only 11 interceptions.

That's where Jurgensen was when Vince Lombardi came on the scene. Observers at the time thought the stern Lombardi would be unable to mold the carefree Jurgensen into a dedicated winner. For in his off-hours, the peerless thrower is known for his lighthearted attitude toward the mores of the football world.

But they were wrong. Jurgensen may give the impression of a grown-up Huckleberry Finn, but he throws a football with accuracy and dedication. Jurgensen was a winner under Lombardi. If he had not hurt his shoulder in 1971, the Redskins might have gone all the way to the Super Bowl.

Jurgensen is a man to be reckoned with on the gridiron. Each season he completes passes of 60 and more yards, and he has the league record of a 99-yarder. He has thrown touchdown passes in 23 straight games. Throughout the 1960's, five times he completed more than 200 passes and gained more than 3,000 yards in single seasons. The league championship has eluded Jurgensen, despite his proven ability. But he sums up his career this way:

"If I had known how frustrating it would be, I might have gone another way. But football can be fun, and it's the thing I do best, so I have few regrets."

Year	Team	Games	Att.	Comp.	Pct.	Yards	TDs	Long	Int.	Pct. Int.	Avg. Gain
1957	Phil.	10	70	33	47.1	470	5	t61	8	11.4	6.71
1958	Phil.	12	22	12	54.5	259	0	61	1	4.5	11.77
1959	Phil.	12	5	3	60.0	27	1	t19	0	0.0	5.40
1960	Phil.	12	44	24	54.5	486	5	71	1	2.3	11.05
1961	Phil.	14	416	235	56.5	3723	32	69	24	5.8	8.95
1962	Phil.	14	366	196	53.6	3261	22	84	26	7.1	8.91
1963	Phil.	9	184	99	53.8	1413	11	t75	13	7.1	7.68
1964	Wash.	14	385	207	53.8	2934	24	t80	13	3.4	7.62
1965	Wash.	13	356	190	53.4	2367	15	t55	16	4.5	6.65
1966	Wash.	14	436	254	58.3	3209	28	t86	19	4.4	7.36
1967	Wash.	14	508	288	56.7	3747	31	t86	16	3.1	7.38
1968	Wash.	12	292	167	57.2	1980	17	t99	11	3.8	6.78
1969	Wash.	14	442	274	62.0	3102	22	t88	15	3.4	7.02
1970	Wash.	14	337	202	59.9	2354	23	t66	10	3.0	6.99
1971	Wash.	5	28	16	57.1	170	0	30	2	7.1	6.07
Totals	**15 yrs.**	**183**	**3891**	**2200**	**56.5**	**29,502**	**236**	**t99**	**175**	**4.5**	**7.58**

Skirts Packers' Ron Kostelnik (77), sent flying by Dave Hill (73) in Super Bowl I contest that Green Bay won.

Len Dawson

Len Dawson
by Joseph Durso

I remember getting up and going out at eight in the morning and playing all day. When I was young, I was small, so I took a beating. But my brothers all played and I had to play, too."

Leonard Ray Dawson reminisced about his childhood in Alliance, Ohio. Born June 20, 1935, he was one of seven sons and four daughters in a family headed by a machinist in a small, tough industrial town.

He was like millions of other youngsters raised in the United States during the Depression years, including Jim Hunt, who came from an equally large family and an equally small town in Texas. When Jim Hunt grew into a 260-pound football player with a rumbling barrel physique that earned him the nickname "Earthquake," he was asked how he got to run so fast. Hunt replied, "I had to, to beat my sisters to the dining-room table."

(Rod Hanna)
Dropping back, Dawson concentrates on watching play unfold.

118

So it was with Lenny Dawson, except that he weighed about eighty pounds less than Jim Hunt and, being "the runt of the litter," learned to live more or less by his wits. His nickname became "Lenny the Cool."

He became a calculating one, all right. As a 14-year-old, he favored baseball over football because he weighed only 125, and he justified his choice by hitting .400 in American Legion ball. Then he played fifth-string football as a sophomore in high school, only to find himself first-string quarterback as a junior, up against mammoth linemen like Cal Jones from Steubenville, who later became a professional star.

"He looked enormous to me," Dawson recalled. "You talk about fear, I had it. But that's when I developed my quick release."

He developed the quick release well enough to complete 100 of 200 passes in high school for 1,615 yards and 19 touchdowns. Then he became the first athlete at Alliance High to make all-state in both football and basketball, got offers from several colleges, and was told it was practically his patriotic duty to choose Ohio State.

But Lenny the Cool noticed that the Buckeyes ran out of the split-T formation and didn't go in for much passing, and observed, "I couldn't see myself running down the line and getting my head torn off."

So he went to Purdue and, when the basketball coach greeted him by exuding, "I know you'll be a big help to us in basketball," Dawson replied, "You don't know that. You've never seen me play."

Later, an assistant football coach greeted him with, "I want to wish you luck." And that time Dawson replied, "You don't need luck, only ability."

There was always "more truth than poetry" in Dawson, even as a youngster. But Lenny the Cool had arrived, and he had the "hot hand" besides. In his first varsity game at Purdue, he completed 11 of 17 passes for four touchdowns against Missouri. A few weeks later, he pitched four more touchdown passes to upset Notre Dame, 27–14. By the time he graduated, he had led the Big Ten in passing three years in a row with 243 completions in 452 passes for 3,325 yards and all-America ranking.

That was the high point. But it was followed shortly by the low points, in droves.

First, he was selected to play on the College All-Stars against the champions of the National Football League, the New York Giants. It was July 26, 1957, and the game was played in Chicago in the heart of Big Ten country before 75,000 fans. But Dawson rode the bench while a pair of quarterbacks named John Brodie and Paul Hornung got the call from Coach Curly Lambeau. The collegians lost, 22–12, with Dawson watching from one of the best seats in the house.

Then he reported to the Pittsburgh Steelers, who had drafted him on the first round, and immediately was assigned second-fiddle by the new coach, Buddy Parker, who already had an old quarterback, Bobby Layne. During the next three seasons, Dawson threw a total of 17 passes.

"Parker never taught me anything," he remembers unhappily. "I was scared and nervous and all screwed-up. He never even told me I was lousy. At least, if he had, he would have shown me he knew I was alive."

Parker knew Dawson was alive, long enough to trade him in 1960 to the Cleveland Browns. But they, too, had a full-time quarterback—Milt Plum. They also had a full-time bench, and Dawson rode it regularly, leaving it sporadically to throw 13 passes one year and 15 the next. So, in his first five seasons as a pro, he had been able to uncork a grand total of 45 passes, and then to reflect:

120

Alan Page of Vikings (88) grabs Dawson, too late to stop him from handing off ball to Mike Garrett, who scampers for score in 2d period of Super Bowl IV.

"I couldn't understand Paul Brown or his system. In his system, a quarterback was just another player. Brown was *it,* first and last. We didn't even have quarterback meetings."

To make matters worse, Dawson was injured in an automobile accident, recovered slowly, and reported to camp overweight. By the end of the 1961 season, he was beginning to have doubts about it all.

"I didn't demand a chance in Pittsburgh and Cleveland," he said, "so perhaps part of not playing was my fault. But I worked hard and waited for an opportunity that never came. I finally began to feel that if two top coaches had observed me a little and were not interested in using me, maybe

I wasn't really good enough. Maybe I was wasting my time and should quit."

That was the lowest low point. There was no place to go but out—or up. But, as luck would have it, Dawson's old assistant coach from Purdue, Hank Stram, had signed on as coach of Lamar Hunt's Dallas Texans of the new American Football League. That fall, Stram was in Pittsburgh for a coaches' convention. He called Dawson and his wife, Jackie, who still lived there.

At dinner, Stram reminisced about the good old days at Purdue and finished with a flourish: "Lenny, if for some reason you ever get your release, I'd love to have you with me."

"I think the general feeling among NFL

121

coaches at the time," Dawson recalled, "was that I did most things fairly well, but didn't have the competitive spark. They thought I was content to serve my time. They thought I couldn't be a winner."

Among those who felt this way was Paul Brown, who also doubted that his bench-riding backup man had a strong arm. Brown agreed to release Dawson if none of the other NFL clubs claimed him, and when they didn't, Stram hustled to Cleveland one night to sign his old college quarterback at the airport.

The five years on the bench had taken their toll, however, and a few more doubts crept in before Dawson got squared away. "I was terrible when I reported," he said. "If my coach had been anyone but Stram, who knew me from the past, I'm sure he would have cut me."

"I was shocked at how bad he was at first," Stram admitted, "but I couldn't help but realize that five years of sitting on the bench or manning the telephones didn't make a man sharp. It really took him a couple of years to get back into the old groove. He was like sterling silver—the silver was still there, but it was tarnished. I'll admit it. If I hadn't known him so well, I might have given up on him. But Lenny was like a baseball pitcher. He never extended himself until he was sure his arm was strong enough. Each day you could see the rotation of the ball becoming a little tighter. I felt secure in my own mind he would make it."

That was in the late summer of 1962, and Dawson was No. 2 behind a quarterback named Cotton Davidson. But in the final exhibition game, he made it at last, and Stram announced that the Texans would open their third season in the AFL with Dawson at quarterback.

Even Horatio Alger couldn't have written a cornier script. Dawson set a league record by completing 61 percent of his passes—189 of 310 for 2,750 yards and 29 touchdowns. The Texans won 11 of their 14 games. And in the playoff for the championship, they defeated Houston (led by George Blanda) in the longest game then on the books: 77 minutes, 54 seconds. The score was 20–17 in two over-time quarters.

Lenny the Cool, with a new convertible as his "Player of the Year" prize and with $2,261.80 in his pocket as his title prize, summed it all up: "After what I had gone through, it had to be the greatest thrill of my life. It was like being reborn."

It also was like being reborn in a different place, because the Texans moved from Dallas to Kansas City the next season, where *they* were reborn as the Chiefs. The adjustment was painful in some ways —the team won only five games that season, and though he led the league with 26 touchdown pitches, Dawson's passing accuracy slipped to 54 per cent. The following year, the Chiefs won seven and lost seven, and the year after that they finished at 7–5–2.

Then, in 1966, everybody was reborn. They won 11 times, lost twice, tied once, and defeated Buffalo for the AFL championship, 31–7, with Dawson completing 16 of 24 passes. Then, on January 15, 1967, Super Bowl I took place in the Los Angeles Coliseum, and in the first match-up between the warring AFL and NFL, Vince Lombardi's Green Bay Packers rolled to a 35–10 victory over the Chiefs.

Despite that pasting, Stram's boys were in business. The AFL was in business, too, as the leagues drew closer in talent and structure. In 1967, the Chiefs finished with a 9–6 record, second to Oakland in the West. In 1968, they tied with Oakland, 12–2, but they were devastated in the playoff, 41–6. And in 1969, just before the leagues merged, they made the AFL playoff as the runner-up in the West under

122

(Rod Hanna)
Dawson zips ball to his target as Dave Hill (73) thwarts Dolphins' Tony Cline from breaking up pass.

UPI
Dawson pegs quickly before defenseman
gets to him; official watches intently.

special rules in effect that year only.

There were a couple more tricks in this Horatio Alger soap-opera, however. The "Dawson jinx" came first. The quarterback, who had broken a thumb at Purdue, also had suffered a bruised hand and broken knuckle in the Chiefs' final preseason workout. Then, in the second game of the schedule, against Boston, he tore the ligaments in his left knee. Five orthopedic surgeons recommended an operation.

"The sixth one said I didn't need an operation," Dawson reported. "He was the one I was looking for. I wasn't 24, I was 34, and knew I wouldn't be playing too

much longer. If I had an operation and didn't play, and we lost, there might not be much future for an old bum-legged quarterback. Besides, I wanted to find out what I'm made of."

He waited six games, returned with a brace on the knee, outpitched Joe Namath and the Jets in New York in the playoff semifinal, then outpitched Daryle Lamonica and the Oakland Raiders. Three years later, the Chiefs were back in the Super Bowl.

They were back with big trouble, though, bigger than the favored Minnesota Vikings. As Super Bowl Week broke over New Orleans, a storm broke over Kansas City: Dawson was mentioned as a friend of a Michigan restaurant man who had been arrested in a nationwide investigation into sports gambling.

To some, it was an echo of an inquiry on the Chiefs three years earlier by the football commissioner's staff, during which Dawson had taken a lie-detector test—and passed. This time, though, he was an established star who had thrown 182 touchdown passes in eight seasons—more than any quarterback in pro ball—and on the eve of the Main Event, he suddenly was under a cloud.

But, with Stram beside him, he walked into press headquarters at the Roosevelt Hotel in New Orleans and read a statement replying to the implication. He had had "a casual acquaintance" with the defendant, Donald Dawson, who was no relation. He had received "calls of sympathy" from him "in recent years," but only about "my knee injuries and the death of my father."

To his teammates, Dawson was "the perfect gentleman," even "the Puritan." But to the 80,977 fans who would be in the Sugar Bowl that day, and the millions who would watch on TV, he was a marked man. If he fumbled or was intercepted, the cynics would have a field day. A flawless game would be his only "out." His roommate, Johnny Robinson, cast an affirmative vote: "If there's anybody who can handle this situation, it's Lenny Dawson."

He handled it. He steered the Chiefs to three field goals, pitched to Otis Taylor for a 46-yard touchdown, completed 12 of 17 passes for 142 yards, and was voted the Most Valuable Player in the game—a game Kansas City won, 23–7, for the championship.

In one sustained stretch of 18 plays, he used 18 formations. Another time, before a kick for the point after touchdown, he advised the referee that the Chiefs wanted the line of scrimmage at the 4-yard line instead of the 2—an option rarely exercised —because the turf was too wet up close for his place-kicker.

"That's how cool Lenny was," said E. J. Holub, the center. "But he's always like that."

"He may be the most accurate passer football has known," said Hank Stram. "He is not a holler-guy, and I've never seen him show great emotion. But he is smart and firm, and leads by example. He is capable of great highs and seldom has excessive lows."

The telephone rang in the jubilant clubhouse. It was a long-distance call from Washington for Lenny Dawson. The quarterback leaned into a little office and said into the phone, "Mr. President, I hope that we'll always try to exemplify what's good in football."

"The entire week was quite an ordeal for me," acknowledged Lenny the Cool. "No one will ever know what I've gone through inside. But the best thing about this game is that we don't have to answer for it for the next three years."

Year	Team	Games	Att.	Comp.	Pct.	Yards	TDs	Long	Int.	Pct. Int.	Avg. Gain
1957	Pitt.	3	4	2	50.0	25	0	15	0	0.0	6.25
1958	Pitt.	4	6	1	16.7	11	0	11	2	33.3	1.83
1959	Pitt.	12	7	3	42.9	60	1	32	0	0.0	8.57
1960	Clev.	2	13	8	61.5	23	0	23	0	0.0	1.77
1961	Clev.	7	15	7	46.7	85	1	t17	3	20.0	5.67
1962	Dal.Tex.	14	310	189	61.0	2759	29	t92	17	5.5	8.90
1963	K.C.	14	352	190	54.0	2389	26	82	19	5.4	6.79
1964	K.C.	14	354	199	56.2	2879	30	72	18	5.1	8.13
1965	K.C.	14	305	163	53.4	2262	21	67	14	4.6	7.42
1966	K.C.	14	284	159	56.0	2527	26	89	10	3.5	8.90
1967	K.C.	14	357	206	57.7	2651	24	t71	17	4.8	7.43
1968	K.C.	14	224	131	58.5	2109	17	t92	9	4.0	9.42
1969	K.C.	9	166	98	59.0	1323	9	t55	13	7.8	7.97
1970	K.C.	13	262	141	53.8	1876	13	t61	14	5.3	7.16
1971	K.C.	14	301	167	55.5	2504	15	82	13	4.3	8.32
Totals 15 yrs.		162	2960	1664	56.2	23,483	212	t92	149	5.0	7.93

As Jets' fans have seen so often, he takes aim and is ready to fire.

Joe Namath

Joe Namath
by Dave Anderson

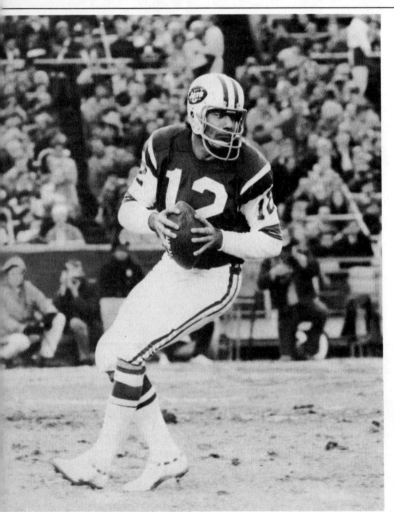

Barton Silverman

On a warm Florida evening, Joe Namath rose to accept an award from the Miami Touchdown Club as the outstanding pro football player of the 1968 season. Three days later, he was to be the quarterback for the New York Jets as they challenged the Baltimore Colts in the Super Bowl game. Now, in his acceptance speech, he began by thanking his parents and family, his high school and college coaches, his Jet coaches and owners, and his teammates. He paused, glanced out at the audience in the red and gold King Arthur's Room of the Miami Springs Villas and took a sip of Scotch from a napkin-wrapped old-fashioned glass.

"You can be the greatest athlete in the world," he continued, "but if you don't win those football games, it doesn't mean anything. And we're going to win Sunday, I'll guarantee you."

(Barton Silverman)
Namath pivots as Jets' offensive linemen make their charge.

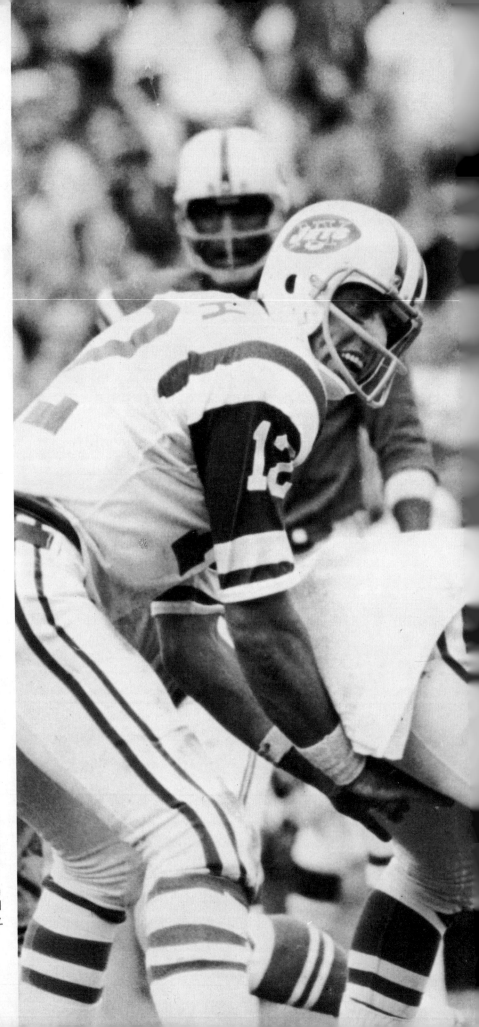

Super Upset Maker

Namath snaps out signals
(right), hands ball to Bill
Mathis (far right, above), as
Bob Talamini leads interference, prepares to pass
(center), as Bubba Smith
leaps up, and is dragged
down by Dennis Gaubatz.

Many people snickered. The Jets were a 17-point underdog. The Colts were considered to have one of the most powerful defensive units in National Football League history. Surely they would swallow the brash young quarterback from the "inferior" American Football League; surely they would invalidate his "guarantee"; surely they would . . .

Except that the Jets won, 16–7.

"There's a whole lot of people changing their minds about us now," Joe Namath said at the Jets' victory party. "Everybody's come up to me tonight, they say, 'I knew you could do it.' Nobody said, 'I didn't think you could do it.' But we didn't win on passing or running, or defense. We won in every phase of the game. If there ever was a world champion, this is it."

And if there ever was a game that transcended its result, this was it.

The outcome shaped the future of pro football. Suddenly the AFL had achieved parity. Several months later, the ten AFL teams, rather than being shuffled among sixteen NFL teams in the merger of the two leagues, retained their identity and were joined by three NFL teams, including the Colts, in what is now the American Conference.

And if there ever was a game that produced a "superstar," that was it.

Joe Namath had suddenly justified his original $427,000 contract with the Jets as a 1965 rookie; in fact, he was a bargain. His stature as a quarterback was further enhanced by a 1971 poll of NFL coaches to determine pro football's most coveted current quarterback in which Joe Namath outdistanced Roman Gabriel of the Los Angeles Rams and John Brodie of the San Francisco 49ers.

"There are two factors in judging a quarterback: preparing for him and playing him," said an AFC coach who requested anonymity. "Joe Namath scares you both times. When you play the Jets, your whole approach to the game involves him. You're so conscious of him, it disrupts your planning. In the game, no matter what the down or distance, he's capable of hitting a big play on you."

But for Joe Namath, the mod bachelor with all those girls and all those wisecracks, football seemed to be merely the stepping-stone to superstardom.

Suddenly, he was appearing as a guest on the big TV shows. He had a role in the motion picture "Norwood." He had business interests: "Broadway Joe's" fast-food chain; an employment agency, in partnership with Mickey Mantle, the retired baseball star. He collaborated on his autobiography, entitled, "I Can't Wait Until Tomorrow—Because I Get Better Looking Every Day."

Almost as suddenly, he retired from football in a dispute with Commissioner Pete Rozelle over alleged "undesirable" customers in Bachelors III, Namath's New York East Side restaurant-nightclub. But he soon surrendered to Rozelle's dictum that he sell his one-third ownership in the bistro. Arriving at training camp a few weeks late, he guided the Jets to the AFL's Eastern Division title. But their loss to the Kansas City Chiefs in the playoffs, 13–6, deprived them of an opportunity to return to the Super Bowl. That loss appeared to haunt Joe Namath, and when the 1970 training camp opened, he didn't report. "I don't want to play football," he said. He had made two more movies, "C. C. Ryder & Co." and "The Last Rebel." He was a celebrity.

He pleaded personal problems. A few weeks later he reconsidered, but even then his enthusiasm had disappeared. In the fifth game of the season—losing to the Colts in spite of Namath's completing 34 of 62 passes—he was slammed into the ground by Billy Ray Smith, one of the

Colts' defensive tackles. He got up, shaking his right wrist. X-rays the next day disclosed a fracture of the navicular bone. His season was over.

Suddenly, when he *couldn't* play, Joe Namath realized that playing was what he really wanted to do.

"When we played the Giants at Shea Stadium, that's the day I remember," he once explained. "Not being able to play just killed me. I wanted to play against the Giants so badly and I couldn't. Even before the game, I had a sad feeling, my eyes were watery. But maybe I was being punished for getting too lackadaisical about football, too nonchalant, taking it for granted. But when you think you're the best at what you do, you want to prove it."

When the 1971 training camp opened, he reported on time, eager to compete. Across the locker room at the Jets' training base at Hofstra University, the quarterback noticed John Schmitt, the center. They shook hands warmly.

"You coming today and leaving?" Schmitt asked, grinning.

"Actually, I've got to go back to Miami," Namath replied, going along with the gag.

"Are you reporting tomorrow?" Schmitt asked.

"No, no. I've got to check on the restaurants down there."

They both laughed. For the Jets, happiness was having their quarterback in training camp on opening day for the first time in three years. And for Joe Namath, happiness was being there. He had discovered that he was a football player. Not a movie actor or a business tycoon, but a football player. That day, as he stuffed five pairs of white football shoes into his locker, he talked about it.

"How many people retire every year in different professions, but come out of retirement? But when an athlete retires and

Namath jumps into air to foil Buffalo Bill defender.

Paying the price, Namath is vulnerable to rush of Pat Holmes of Oilers.

comes back, it's a big thing. But athletes are like anybody else. They get tired of their jobs, or they have emotional problems. They're entitled to change their opinion or their feelings. And once I got back into it last season, it was taken away from me by my wrist. I missed it."

During the workouts, he wore white football pants with the smiling-face symbol he had drawn on the left knee—a circle surrounding two dots for the eyes, a curved line for the mouth.

"Maybe the smile is the reason my left knee feels so good," he declared about a week before the Jets' opening exhibition game. "I used to have a sharp pain in my left knee every time I got set to throw, but it's felt great so far."

In the opening exhibition, though, another pain occurred, wiping the smile off the left knee.

It happened while the Jets were demolishing the Detroit Lions, 14–0, in the second quarter at the Tampa (Florida) Stadium. Namath had completed seven of thirteen passes for 116 yards. But deep in Jets' territory, he called a running play on which Lee White was to sweep right end. White fumbled. Mike Lucci, a Lion linebacker, scooped up the loose ball at the Jets' 29-yard line and rumbled toward the goalline. As a high school star in Beaver Falls, Pennsylvania, Namath had been a defensive back, and at the University of Alabama, he had occasionally played defense. Following his instincts, he attempted to tackle the 230-pound Lion linebacker, but missed the tackle. As he sprawled on the grass, his left knee extended, he was hit there by the helmet of Paul Naumoff, another Lion linebacker. Namath grabbed his knee. Naumoff bent over him.

"You all right, Joe?" the Lion linebacker asked. "You all right?"

Namath knew he wasn't. Hopping weakly to the sideline, he was met by Dr.

James A. Nicholas, the orthopedic specialist who had performed three previous operations on his knee.

"It's not like anything else," Namath said. "It's bad. It's slipping. It's numb."

Immediate surgery was required. Once again, Joe Namath was deprived of playing football, only this time he was accorded sympathy because of his changed attitude. His image as a playboy and wise guy had once provoked some fans into voicing hopes that he would be clobbered. But now the news of the accident that flashed throughout the nation that Saturday night saddened most people, particularly his Jet teammates. With him, they had hoped to return to the Super Bowl. Without him, they knew they couldn't. Although they had been aware of his artistry as a passer from the day he arrived as a $427,000 rookie, their faith in him had been solidified in their Super Bowl victory following the 1968 season.

When the Jets had first heard of the deal for their new teammate, they wondered if anybody could be worth that kind of money. At the time, the AFL was in a bidding war with the NFL for the best rookies. The Jets had drafted Namath, as had the St. Louis Cardinals of the NFL, but when the price kept going up, the Cardinals dropped out.

This was his original contract, as disclosed by Dick Young of the New York *Daily News*:

1965 salary	$25,000
1966 salary	$25,000
1967 salary	$25,000
1968 option year (minimum)	$25,000
Bonus (deferred payments)	$200,000
Lawyers fee (10%)	$30,000
Lincoln Continental	$7,000
Total	$337,000

In addition, two of Namath's brothers, Bob and Frank, and a brother-in-law, each received $30,000 over three years, allegedly to act as Jet scouts in the Beaver Falls, Pennsylvania, area. The $90,000, added to Joe's $337,000, brought the final sum to $427,000.

"But if I didn't have my lawyer [Mike Bite] and some other good people around me," Namath said at the time, "I'd have signed for almost anything."

Joe Namath had simply wanted to play pro football. Born on May 31, 1943, he had been a football, baseball, and basketball star as a boy in Beaver Falls, where his father worked in a steel mill. His football coach was Larry Bruno, a man he always credits with first developing his natural talents.

"He was some coach," Joe once said. "In my senior year I completed 84 out of 120 passes, and not one time did I get hit behind the line. Eleven guys on that team got scholarships."

Joe's scholarship took him to Alabama, where Coach Paul ("Bear") Bryant sculptured him into the $427,000 rookie quarterback. But what Namath didn't realize at first was that he didn't know everything about being a quarterback. In his cool, self-satisfied manner, he thought he could move right in with the pros and excel. After all, it was football. And he had been playing football all his life.

But it wasn't that simple.

One day, when he was a rookie in training camp, the Jets were running through plays and he came out of the huddle, hunched over the center, and began to call signals.

"Set, 46, 32 . . . ahhh-h!"

He walked away from the center and Weeb Ewbank, the Jet coach, looked at him.

"What happened?" Ewbank said.

"I blew it," Namath replied. "I blew the play. I called the wrong formation."

"All right," Ewbank said patiently. "That's all right."

Ewbank's patience and understanding were important, although Namath probably didn't appreciate it at the time. Ewbank, who had developed Johnny Unitas a decade earlier, knew a quarterback when he saw one. He knew, too, what a quarterback had to do, and how he should do it. At one workout as a rookie, Namath let go a long pass down the sideline to Don Maynard that seemed about to soar over the old red-brick buildings of the Peekskill (N.Y.) Military Academy where the Jets were training.

"You don't have to show me your arm," said Ewbank quietly. "If you couldn't throw, you wouldn't be here."

In one of his first workouts, Namath missed several receivers. He underthrew some. He overthrew others. Finally, he turned to Ewbank.

"Don't worry, coach," he said. "When I get warmed up, I'll hit all those guys."

Midway in his rookie season, he was warmed up. In his third season, in 1967, his passes produced 4,007 yards. No other quarterback had passed for more than the 3,747 accumulated by Sonny Jurgensen of the Washington Redskins the same year. Jurgensen had put together 3,732 yards in 1961 for the previous record. In the next-to-last game of his 4,007-yard season, Namath suffered a fractured right cheekbone when he was swatted by Ben Davidson, the Oakland Raiders' huge pass rusher.

"We'll play next week," Dr. Nicholas said. "We'll fix him up with a special helmet."

Namath, knowing he wouldn't have to rejoin the Jets in San Diego until the following Tuesday, stood in the lobby of their Oakland motel. He was wearing a tuxedo and was about to leave for Las Vegas to relax.

"It's hard to chew," he was telling peo-ple, "but I can play in San Diego. I'll be there."

The next season, his teammates on the offensive unit voted him their captain before the opener in Kansas City, which made it a virtual mandate. He responded by guiding the offensive unit to a 70-yard ball-control drive against the Chiefs in the final six minutes to preserve a 20–19 victory. On the Jets' chartered airliner to New York that night, he strolled into the first-class section to rehash the successful strategy with Ewbank.

"That's the first time Joe has ever come up front like that," one of the Jets' assistant coaches remarked. "Maybe the captaincy has made him a leader."

It had. But when the Buffalo Bills and the Denver Broncos each intercepted five of his passes to generate upsets of the Jets, Namath was annoyed at being victimized by inferior teams. After the loss to the Broncos at Shea Stadium, he arrived at his locker with a stern expression.

"I ain't saying nothin'," he announced, "except that I stink."

After that, he changed his style. He didn't throw a touchdown pass during the next four games, but the Jets won them all.

"I disciplined myself," he later confessed. "I remembered an old rule that the only way to win is to keep from losing."

But in the AFL championship game with Oakland, another interception jeopardized the Jets' opportunity to qualify for the Super Bowl game. The Raiders had moved ahead, 23–20, on the touchdown provided by that interception. Now Namath was confronted with the most critical situation in his celebrated career. Unless he guided the Jets to another score, he would be thought of as overrated, and worse, as overpaid.

Provided with a decent field position at

UPI
Namath in classic motion as Jets try to hold back Bills.

Namath steps back, making a split-second decision on where he should pass.

the Jets' 32-yard line after the kickoff return, Namath connected with wide receiver George Sauer at the left sideline for a first down at the 42. On the next play, he flung a long arching pass to his other wide receiver, Don Maynard, that traveled about 75 yards in the air from the left hashmark to the right sideline. Maynard caught it

at the Raiders' 10 and was dragged down on the 6. First down, goal to go.

In the huddle, Namath decided on a roll-out to his left, with running back Bill Mathis the intended receiver on a flare pass. But the strong Raider pass-rush disrupted Namath's plan. Aware that Mathis was covered, he glanced at Sauer, then at tight end Pete Lammons, but both were covered. Quickly, his eyes fanning to the right, he found Maynard in the end zone with several Raiders surrounding him. With the quick release of an archer's bow, he arrowed the ball to the veteran wide receiver.

"I heard that ball hum," running back Matt Snell would say later. "I heard that ball go by me."

The next thing Snell heard was the roar from 62,627 spectators. Maynard had caught the pass, the force of it knocking him to his knees in the cold, brown dirt of the end zone. With three passes for a total of 68 yards, Namath had produced a touchdown in 55 seconds. And that touchdown for a 27–23 victory clinched the AFL title for the Jets and qualified them for their Super Bowl game.

"But you have to be lucky to win the Super Bowl, too," Namath has acknowledged. "You have to avoid injuries."

Until the 1970 season, despite his fragile knees, he had been lucky enough to play in every Jets' game of his career. But then the factured bone in his wrist stopped him. Later, in 1971, when knee surgery prevented him from returning until late in the season, he wrote another of his dramatic scenarios.

The Jets were playing the 49ers at Shea Stadium when Bob Davis, their interim quarterback, was flattened by the San Fran-cisco linemen, and suffered a sprained ankle.

"I said to myself," Namath disclosed later, " 'Well, you got to go in now.' When you hear all that noise, naturally, I was excited. I was hoping I'd lift the team. You have to have confidence. When I went in there, I said, 'We're going to go now.' "

And the Jets went. Namath threw three touchdown passes, but his final-minute pass from the 19-yard line was intercepted in the end zone, and the Jets lost, 24–21. In the locker room, the disappointed quarterback was greeted by his father, John Namath.

"Terrific!" his father said.

"We didn't win," Joe replied.

Typically, he minimized the value of his eleven completions in twenty-seven attempts for 258 yards. But two weeks later, he guided the Jets to a 13–6 victory over the New England Patriots, his first winning game in more than a year.

"You're a winning quarterback," somebody told him.

"What do you mean?" Namath asked, apparently confused.

"You're a winning quarterback. This is the first game you've won in more than a year."

Joe Namath smiled slowly.

"I may not have a lot of victories," he said, "but I'm always a winning quarterback."

Year	Team	Games	Att.	Comp.	Pct.	Yards	TDs	Long	Int.	Pct. Int.	Avg. Gain
1965	N.Y.J.	13	340	164	48.2	2220	18	62	15	4.4	6.53
1966	N.Y.J.	14	471	232	49.3	3379	19	t77	27	5.7	7.17
1967	N.Y.J.	14	491	258	52.3	4007	26	t75	28	5.7	8.16
1968	N.Y.J.	14	380	187	49.2	3147	15	t87	17	4.5	8.28
1969	N.Y.J.	14	361	185	51.2	2734	19	t60	17	4.7	7.57
1970	N.Y.J.	5	179	90	50.3	1259	5	t72	12	6.7	7.03
1971	N.Y.J.	4	59	28	47.5	537	5	t74	6	10.2	9.10
Totals	**7 yrs.**	**78**	**2281**	**1144**	**50.2**	**17,283**	**107**	**t87**	**122**	**5.3**	**7.58**

Eyes gesturing Giants' rusher as he winds up to throw the long bomb.

John Brodie

John Brodie

by Frank Litsky

W hen John Brodie does things, he does them with a flourish.

He was voted the most valuable player in the 1956 East-West Shrine game and the 1957 New York Giants-College All-Stars game. These were mighty achievements in a vintage year that produced such all-Americans and future professional stars as Jim Brown, Paul Hornung, Tommy McDonald, Alex Karras, Lou Michaels, Ron Kramer, and Jerry Tubbs.

He has survived the bumps and bruises that have made pro football a classroom for orthopedic surgeons, and he has lived to play another day. He has passed for almost seventeen miles, more than any other National Football League quarterback in history except for Johnny Unitas.

Brodie started his pro career in 1957, the year that Joe Namath entered Beaver

UPI
Brodie side-arms pass to avoid Bears' Willie Holman in game in which 49ers' star joined exclusive 2,000th Completion Club.

142

Falls (Pennsylvania) High School. That was also the year that Sonny Jurgensen and Len Dawson were rookies, and Johnny Unitas, Bart Starr and Earl Morrall were second-year men. How does Brodie stand in this collection of geriatric marvels?

"He has to rank 1–2–3 with football's best passers," said Dick Nolan, Brodie's coach with the San Francisco 49ers. Said Coach Tom Landry of the Dallas Cowboys, "I marvel at the way he has mastered quarterbacking."

Glittering statistics and praise have never made Brodie content.

"I guess you are never known as a great quarterback," he once said, "unless you win a championship." He has done everything else. In 1965, when the 49ers led the NFL in scoring and Brodie made the all-pro team, they barely finished above .500. In 1970, when Brodie led the National Football Conference in most touchdown passes and fewest interceptions and was voted NFC player of the year, the 49ers lost to the Cowboys in the NFC championship game. In 1971, the 49ers again won their division title, only to lose to the Cowboys again in the conference championship playoff.

Brodie took those two defeats badly. He had worked too hard and too long to accept such setbacks.

"Being a pro quarterback," said Brodie, "is a big commitment. You put in important years."

Brodie has put in the years. He has always been poised, outgoing and charming —the prototype of a happy Californian. Though his hair is thinning, he is still handsome, full of confidence, and always in command of the situation. He has kept his cool under all sorts of fire, on the gridiron and off. In 1966 these qualities made him a millionaire quarterback.

The war between the established NFL and the upstart American Football League had heated almost to the boiling point. The leagues, bidding against each other, were paying all sorts of bonuses to untested players fresh out of college. In 1965, the New York Jets of the AFL gave $427,000 to Joe Namath, a quarterback from the University of Alabama. In 1966, the Atlanta Falcons of the NFL landed linebacker Tommy Nobis of the University of Texas for $600,000 (the Houston Oilers of the AFL were ready to go even higher), and the Green Bay Packers of the NFL signed halfback Donny Anderson of Texas A. and M. for $711,000.

But the established players were not so fortunate. They had started at a low salary and their small annual raises had kept their earnings comparatively low. For example, in his big year of 1965, John Brodie earned $35,000—the average wage for a good quarterback on a non-championship team. For his $35,000 he led the NFL in completions, completion percentage, passing yardage, and touchdown passes. He asked for $65,000 for the 1966 season. The 49ers swallowed hard and wouldn't say yes or no, or even offer to compromise.

Meanwhile, the NFL and AFL were embarked upon what threatened to become a double-suicide pact, and no one seemed to know how to save the day. Finally, the AFL shelved Milt Woodard, its pleasant but ineffective commissioner, and replaced him with Al Davis, coach of the Oakland Raiders. The thirty-seven-year-old Davis was a clever man who knew how to get things done. The AFL owners gave him something to do—end the war. They also gave him a war chest.

At that point, the NFL was by far the stronger league. NFL people liked to say that a major reason for their league's superiority was its quarterbacks.

Davis made a bold decision. He decided to attack the NFL by raiding, and his target was quarterbacks. Instead of

(Frank Rippon)

Brodie gallops away from line of scrimmage while he searches for an eligible San Francisco player.

Frank Rippon
Jack Gregory of Cleveland lands at Brodie's feet while he prepares to pass.

throwing away hundreds of thousands of dollars on rookies who might never make it, he reasoned, why not give the same money to quarterbacks who had proved themselves? If his plan succeeded, the NFL would call a truce, lest it run out of quarterbacks.

Davis's first target was Roman Gabriel of the Los Angeles Rams. Gabriel agreed to jump to the other league and accepted a $100,000 down payment. Word spread quickly via the grapevine, and Davis's telephone started ringing as NFL veterans reached out for a piece of the pie.

By this time, the NFL and AFL owners were meeting in merger talks, and every time another NFL quarterback's name dribbled out of the rumor mill, the NFL became a little more anxious for peace. Within days, six other NFL quarterbacks were said to be ready to sign with the AFL. Among them were Sonny Jurgensen of the Washington Redskins, Fran Tarkenton, then with the Minnesota Vikings, and John Brodie.

Davis had assigned Don Klosterman, the dynamic young general manager of the Houston Oilers, to recruit Brodie. Klosterman was representing his league, not his team, although it was generally assumed that Brodie would be assigned to Houston.

Klosterman offered Brodie $750,000 over ten years, though he would have to play only five years. He wrote the figures on a memo pad. Brodie tore off the piece of paper and put it in his pocket. He telephoned the 49ers to tell them he was leaving them, and they asked him to wait until they called back. The merger talks were going hot and heavy, and the 49ers hoped to save their quarterback.

Brodie waited. He asked Klosterman to put his signature on the note. Klosterman declined. Brodie put the paper back in his pocket and went home. Later, as he was playing golf at Lake Tahoe, he heard about

UPI

Brodie goes back to pass—a familiar sight
to San Francisco 49er followers.

the merger. "Somebody owes me $750,-
000," he said.

Brodie hired a lawyer, who promptly
said he would settle for $1,000,000 plus
$100,000 in legal fees. If Brodie didn't get
the money, the lawyer said, they would sue
for treble damages. The two leagues, now
committed to a shotgun marriage, feared
a law suit. Even if they won, they were
afraid that Congress would frown on a bill
allowing the leagues to hold a common
player draft, and without a common draft
there could be no merger.

So the leagues offered Brodie $750,000
plus $50,000 in legal fees, with Brodie re-
turning to the 49ers. Not enough, the
lawyer said, and he sent Brodie and his
family to Hawaii to await a better offer.
While the other 49ers were starting the
rigors of training camp, Brodie waited.
Finally, he signed for $921,000 over
twelve years plus $75,000 for his lawyer.
Brodie was guaranteed $75,000 a year for
playing in 1966, 1967, and 1968; $90,000
in 1969; and $81,000 in 1970. In addition,
when he retired, he would collect $75,000

a year for seven years. The 49ers would
pay almost sixty percent of the total and
the other twenty-three NFL and AFL
teams would pay the rest.

Brodie was fined $3,000 for reporting
late to camp. On his first day, center Bruce
Bosley snapped the ball, Brodie faded,
looked at the ball and laughed. It was not
a ball, but a pineapple. Painted on it was
"$1,000,000 less $4,000." Brodie could indeed afford to laugh.

Laughter has always come easily to
John Brodie. From his days at Oakland
Technical High School, across the bay
from San Francisco, he has done most
things better than other people.

In high school, he played football, basketball, and baseball. He entered Stanford
University without an athletic scholarship
because he wanted to be free to play golf
in the spring, and his family could afford
it. As a freshman quarterback, he impressed no one. As a sophomore, he recalled, "I was so darn bad, they tried to get
rid of me." As a junior, he was ninth in
the nation in total offense, he punted, and
he played safety on defense. As a senior,
he led the country in total offense. He ran
only out of necessity ("I had to run if I
wanted to stay alive," he said). The 49ers
drafted him on the first round.

In Brodie's rookie year of 1957, the
49er quarterback was Y. A. Tittle, almost
thirty-one years old, but with his best playing years ahead (for the New York Giants,
not the 49ers). For four years, Brodie
played—when he got into the game—in
Tittle's shadow.

A turning point came in 1960. Red
Hickey, the 49er coach, looking for a
wrinkle to beat a superior Baltimore Colts
team, devised the shotgun offense. The two
ends were split, two running backs were
slotted or winged, and the third running
back was flanked outside an end. The quarterback lined up five yards behind the center. He had five potential pass receivers,

which was good, but no blocking back, which was dangerous. The quarterback had to be ready to run, and Tittle was no runner. Brodie could run, though he didn't like to.

The 49ers, with their new formation, upset the Colts and won three of their last four games, mostly with the shotgun. Brodie averaged 9.5 yards per running play, though, as Jim Murray wrote in the Los Angeles *Times,* "Brodie runs like fourth-class mail."

Tittle was traded away after the 1960 season. In 1961, the shotgun got a new twist—alternating quarterbacks. In a passing situation, Brodie would be the quarterback. In a running situation, he was replaced by Bill Kilmer, a rookie who had been an all-American tailback at UCLA.

For five weeks, the 49ers averaged 33 points per game, with the NFL's top offense. Then the Chicago Bears destroyed the shotgun. Bill George, the Bears' superb middle linebacker, lined up over the center and racked up the quarterback on every play—whether pass or run. Three games later, the 49ers abandoned the shotgun.

Brodie willingly became a T-formation quarterback again. He held the job for the next decade, except for 1963, when he broke an arm in an automobile accident and was absent for most of the season. Year in and year out, despite a team that sometimes lacked a running attack and sometimes good pass blocking, he was the model of a pro quarterback.

He was also the model of a golfer. Four years and two lessons after he had taken up the game, he shot a 64 on a par-70 course in Hayden Lake, Idaho ("A fairly easy course," he said). He shot a 67 on the celebrated Monterey Peninsula course, duly impressing his playing partner, Bing Crosby.

Brodie played down his golf achievements. "After all," he said, "I played every day for at least six months a year, which is more than most people play in a lifetime." But he played at scratch, and for two winters and springs he played on the pro tour.

One day, during an exhibition at Seattle, three thousand spectators tagged along. "I guess I'm a pretty popular golfer to draw a crowd like this," he said. "You sure are," said his playing partner, Arnold Palmer.

Year	Team	Games	Att.	Comp.	Pct.	Yards	TDs	Long	Int.	Pct. Int.	Avg. Gain
1957	S.F.	5	21	11	52.4	160	2	28	3	14.3	7.62
1958	S.F.	12	172	103	59.9	1224	6	61	61	7.6	7.12
1959	S.F.	12	64	30	46.9	354	2	34	7	10.9	5.53
1960	S.F.	11	207	103	49.8	1111	6	t65	9	4.3	5.37
1961	S.F.	14	283	155	54.8	2588	14	t70	12	4.2	9.14
1962	S.F.	14	304	175	57.6	2272	18	t80	16	5.3	7.47
1963	S.F.	3	61	30	49.2	367	3	t44	4	6.6	6.02
1964	S.F.	14	392	193	49.2	2498	14	t83	16	4.1	6.37
1965	S.F.	13	391	242	61.9	3112	30	t59	16	4.1	7.96
1966	S.F.	14	427	232	54.3	2810	16	t65	22	5.2	6.58
1967	S.F.	14	349	168	48.1	2013	11	t63	16	4.6	5.77
1968	S.F.	14	404	234	57.9	3020	22	t65	21	5.2	7.48
1969	S.F.	12	347	194	55.9	2405	16	t80	15	4.3	6.93
1970	S.F.	14	378	223	59.0	2941	24	t79	10	2.6	7.78
1971	S.F.	14	387	208	53.7	2642	18	t71	24	6.2	6.83
Totals 15 yrs.		180	4187	2301	55.0	29,517	202	t83	204	4.9	7.05

Noted for his strength, he is able to ignore grasping arms of a Giant defender and approaching Fred Dryer and will complete play as planned.

Roman Gabriel

Roman Gabriel

by George DeGregorio

When Roman Gabriel played football at New Hanover High School in Wilmington, North Carolina, he was constantly aware that he was playing in the shadow of New Hanover's favorite son, Sonny Jurgensen, who had gone on to stardom at Duke University and in the National Football League. It was there that he decided to live up to the standards of excellence other people set for him.

Gabriel, the son of a Filipino laborer who immigrated to the United States in 1925, was a sensitive, shy athlete, and in many ways a loner. As a worker in railroad dining cars, his father couldn't afford to send him to college, but Roman distinguished himself on the local gridiron, just as Jurgensen had, and won scholarships to colleges throughout the nation.

"Without an athletic scholarship, there

Gabriel veers to his left at full speed to evade Kermit Alexander of 49ers and makes sizable gain.

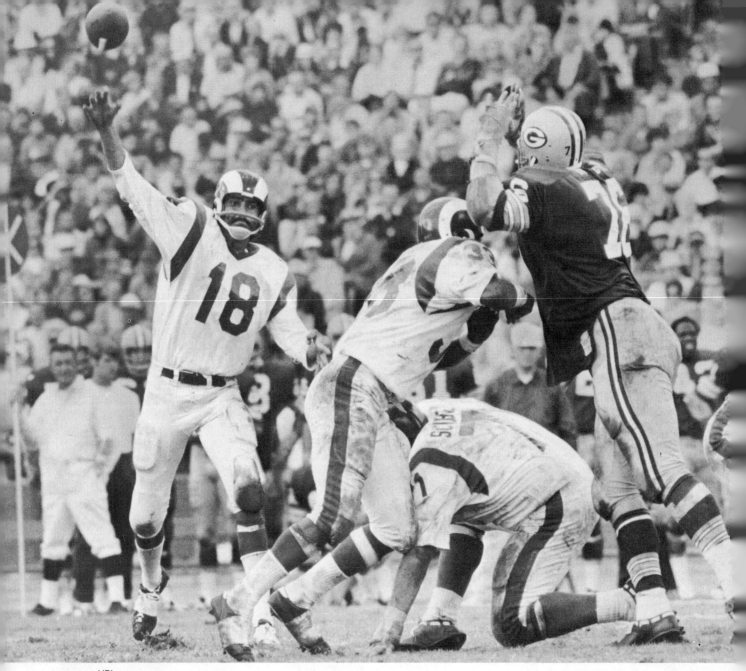

Gabriel's blockers keep out Mike McCoy (76) of Green Bay to give him time to pass.

would have been no college. We couldn't afford it," he has said.

At North Carolina State, he went on to all-America fame and was scouted extensively by all the pro clubs. In 1962 he was the number one draft choice of the Los Angeles Rams. By 1971, after ten seasons with the Rams, Roman Gabriel had risen against long odds to the front rank of professional football quarterbacks.

His passing record of 1,540 completions in 2,990 attempts for 20,196 yards and 142

touchdowns (25 in one season) had surpassed even those of two former Rams—Bob Waterfield and Norm Van Brocklin. Both players are in pro football's Hall of Fame.

But the path to success for Gabriel was not laid out with a red carpet. Before he got a chance to prove his ability, Gabriel experienced self-doubt, frustration and mediocre coaching.

He joined the Rams in 1962 with the expectation of playing under and learning

154

from a master, Bob Waterfield, then the coach of the very club he, as a rookie, had led to a world championship in 1945.

"I figured he was a great passer, and I would be able to learn under him," Gabriel later said of Waterfield.

But his expectations soon turned to disillusion. The stardom and fame he had enjoyed at college now seemed merely tinsel to be cast aside for the bigger game of making it as a professional.

Gabriel was seeking a tutor and father figure to guide him to a distinguished place among football's great quarterbacks. (Despite his shyness and sensitive nature, Gabriel never doubted his innate skill as a player.) But Waterfield was not that kind of a coach.

"Waterfield never taught me a thing," Gabriel has said. "He'd say, 'Stand around and watch.' He never told me anything, play-wise. We played the Redskins in a preseason game. 'Here,' Waterfield said. He handed me four plays. 'Learn these.' That was that."

By the time the Rams had played eight games that season, Waterfield was dismissed. But even that did not help Gabriel. Waterfield's successor, Harland ("Swede") Svare, admired Gabriel's strength, but found him deficient as a pro quarterback.

Sitting on the bench became unbearable for Gabriel. The change from campus star to obscure second-stringer was more than he could take. His sullen attitude was evident to everyone on the team.

Like Waterfield, Svare sometimes discussed Gabriel's "shortcomings" with the press, who reported them to the fans.

Their indictment of Gabriel read like this: Gabriel throws too hard; Gabriel throws too soft; Gabriel can't throw a spiral; Gabriel is inaccurate. They might have added that Gabriel blows his top, but the young man was not about to have them carry him out in a straitjacket. He would bide his time and make his way.

What irritated Gabriel most was that he wasn't learning the game. "I used to practice by myself," he has said. "I'd throw the ball, and then run and pick it up, and throw it back. That was my practice. As a result, I didn't know how to play pro football."

During this time the Rams, in spite of their coaches' knowledge of Gabriel's deficiencies, were losers. They were considered the breather on the schedules of their opponents. In Gabriel's first season the Rams posted a 1–12–1 record. Their quarterbacks, besides Gabriel, were hot-and-cold performers such as Zeke Bratkowski, Ron Miller, Bill Munson and Terry Baker.

When Gabriel finally got a chance under Svare, he virtually became a laughingstock. The coaches sent in all the plays to him and Gabriel consequently became known as Roman the Robot, something he would find hard to live down for several seasons.

"It was humiliating," Gabriel has recalled. "In the old days I was not allowed to audibilize. If you cannot audibilize in this game, you're dead."

Like Bart Starr of the Green Bay Packers, he bore the slings and arrows for a time and then issued an ultimatum: "Play me or trade me." He signed with the rival American Football League's Oakland team for a four-year $400,000 contract at about the time George Allen came to coach the Rams in 1966. Allen's arrival, and the eventual merger of the leagues, enabled Gabriel to void his pact with the Raiders and stay with the Rams.

Unlike Starr, whose early days with Vince Lombardi were strained, Gabriel was sympatico with Allen from the start. The relationship was apparently what the Rams needed, for they became almost instant winners.

Allen proved to be the father image, the mentor, Gabriel had been looking for. The two complemented each other in terms of the game's work-ethic cliches. Allen's prescription: "You have to want to sacrifice and pay the price to be a champion." Gabriel's principle: "I always apply myself 110 percent. To operate at 100 percent is easy."

Allen saw qualities in Gabriel that Waterfield and Svare were incapable of seeing or were unwilling to see. Gabriel is acknowledged to be the biggest and strongest quarterback in the history of pro football. His six-foot-four-inch, 225-pound frame is a testament to his physical prowess. He confronts the blitz by stiff-arming the 250-pounders who rush in to annihilate him.

His stiff-arming ability and his strength give him valuable extra time to survey his receivers and throw the ball, even with defensemen grasping at him.

In the T-formation his strength gives the Rams an advantage in the traditional ratio (11-10) of tacklers to blockers. Normally, in devising offensive patterns, teams automatically remove the quarterback from the play pattern because he is either passing or handing off. That always leaves a potential tackler who cannot be mathematically accounted for in the blocking pattern. But Gabriel's brawn gives the Rams the equivalent of an extra blocker.

Gabriel also has tremendous passing range. He is capable of throwing the ball eighty yards. And he has one of the best winning records among the quarterbacks in NFL history, although at this writing he and the Rams have missed the big prize, a conference title that would put them in the Super Bowl class.

From the time he took over the playcalling in Allen's first year, Gabriel has kept the Rams on the winning side of the ledger. In 1966 they reversed a 4-10-0 mark of the previous season to an 8-6-0,

their first plus season in seven years. In 1967 their 11-1-2 record earned them a division title and a bid for the Western Conference championship.

Gabriel was the architect of the Rams' record fourteen-game winning streak that extended over two seasons—the last eight games of 1967 and the first six of 1968. From 1966 through 1971, Gabriel etched a Ram record of fifty-seven victories, twenty-two defeats, five ties, two Coastal Division championships, and two Playoff Bowl triumphs. In effect, Gabriel won three out of every four games he directed. Gabriel's interception percentage of 3.3 is the lowest in the NFL and his 206 consecutive passes without a theft is the third best mark in league history.

The fact that Gabriel has not been able to get his team over the big hurdle and into the Super Bowl troubles him. Yet he is a quarterback with the credentials that stand with the best and this was recognized by his peers, the NFL players, when they voted him the most valuable player of 1966.

He received the award only days before the Rams were to meet the Minnesota Vikings for the Western Conference championship. Gabriel had started the season deeply aware of the "runner-up" label the experts were pinning on the Rams. He had said before the campaign, "If we come in second again, we could get rooted into the philosophy of being a second-place team. This year is a breaking point."

The Rams lost that game, 23-30, and the title. Joe Kapp, himself a highly volatile and controversial player, drove the Vikings 65 yards in the fourth period for the clinching touchdown after the Rams had led, 17-7, in the first half.

During the game Gabriel was thrown for a safety by Carl Eller, the Vikings' all-pro defender. Gabriel claimed later that film clips showed Eller had stopped him at the one and then pushed him into the end zone. Sprawled in the dressing room, still depressed ninety minutes after the game, Gabriel explained, "I've played eight years in the NFL now and I've played in two playoff games. We've lost both times. I'm not saying I'm going to quit. The only thing I'm saying is that I've got to sit down and have a talk with myself. I'm not going to go on playing if I think I'm hurting this team. Losing makes you wonder about yourself."

Gabriel's loyalty to Allen, and the extent to which he was willing to show it, was displayed in the last week of December, 1968, when the Rams announced the dismissal of Allen. A "personality" conflict had escalated between Allen and George Reeves, then the owner of the club.

Shaken by the possible loss of his father figure, Gabriel polled the players by telephone to enlist support for Allen. He succeeded in getting a large majority to support the coach publicly. With Gabriel in the vanguard, many of them showed up at a West Coast news conference at which Allen told his side of the story. The players'

outspoken backing of Allen (some threatened to quit the team or asked to be traded, and Gabriel said he would only play where Allen coached) made Reeves have a change of heart. Within a week he patched things up with Allen and rehired him.

It seemed only fitting for Gabriel to be instrumental in saving the job of the coach, who more than any other individual had given him the opportunity to become one of the best quarterbacks in football. The club did not renew Allen's contract after the 1970 season, however, and he went off to Washington to help rebuild the Redskins.

The new man to nurse Roman Gabriel's fortunes in 1971 was Tommy Prothro, a highly successful coach at UCLA. Gabriel continued to throw his passes as if from a slingshot, completing 180 of 352 attempts for 2,238 yards and 17 touchdowns, but the Rams, alas, finished second again—losing to the 49ers—with an 8–5–1 record. For the fourth time, though, Gabriel was named the Rams' most valuable player by Ye Old Rams, an organization of former Ram players.

Year	Team	Games	Att.	Comp.	Pct.	Yards	TDs	Long	Int.	Pct. Int.	Avg. Gain
1962	L.A.	6	101	57	56.4	670	3	65	2	2.0	6.63
1963	L.A.	12	281	130	46.3	1947	8	t77	11	3.9	6.93
1964	L.A.	7	143	65	45.5	1236	9	t70	5	3.5	8.64
1965	L.A.	7	173	83	48.0	1321	11	t60	5	2.9	7.64
1966	L.A.	14	397	217	54.7	2540	10	t84	16	4.0	6.40
1967	L.A.	14	371	196	52.8	2779	25	t80	13	3.5	7.49
1968	L.A.	14	366	184	50.3	2364	19	t60	16	4.4	6.46
1969	L.A.	14	399	217	54.4	2549	24	t93	7	1.8	6.39
1970	L.A.	14	407	211	51.8	2552	16	71	12	2.9	6.27
1971	L.A.	14	352	180	51.1	2238	17	68	10	2.8	6.36
Totals 10 yrs.		116	2990	1540	51.5	20,196	142	t93	97	3.2	6.75